Ryan Craig

FILTHY BUSINESS

T0347910

OBERON BOOKS
LONDON

WWW.OBERONBOOKS.COM

First published in 2017 by Oberon Books Ltd
521 Caledonian Road, London N7 9RH
Tel: +44 (0) 20 7607 3637 / Fax: +44 (0) 20 7607 3629
e-mail: info@oberonbooks.com
www.oberonbooks.com

A catalogue record for this book is available from the British
Library.

PB ISBN: 9781786821621
E ISBN: 9781786821638

Foreword

There was usually a point in the school holidays when my father, finally exasperated by my aimless lolloping about the house, insisted I come into work with him. He ran a mattress, bed and foam rubber shop on the Holloway Road. It was a family business. My father had started on the markets in his early teens working alongside his cousin, father, uncles, and grandfather, who'd created the business from off-cuts he'd collected working as a tyre-fitter in a tram factory. He'd met and married my great-grandmother in London, but both had arrived as Jewish refugees from Eastern Europe at the beginning of the 20th century. They began the business from their house in Stepney and, with their four sons, sold bits of rubber on markets in Leather Lane, Lower Marsh, and Dalston Waste. These market people were, out of necessity, tough, inventive, volatile characters, and as the business and the family grew to dominate the retailing of rubber in the 50s and 60s, tempers were easily ignited and the firm and its power struggles became legendary. By the time of my appearance there in the late 1980s my father had struck out on his own and ran a shop with a staff of around eight or nine. This included my grandfather and great uncle, a couple of men called John who carried, cut, stuffed, and sold, some drivers/humpers, an Iraqi bookkeeper, and, in the basement, a couple of machinists – a sister of one of the Johns and a Nigerian émigré. All these busy people politely tolerated me, but, in truth I was entirely useless. I couldn't sell, I couldn't measure, I couldn't wrap, all I could do was aimlessly lollop about. I do, though, vividly remember the shop; its petroleum stench and the teeming chaos of the oozing Dexion shelves and the heaving stockroom and the dog-eared order books and, everywhere, the piles and piles and piles of foam rubber. I remember the euphoria of the big sale or the new idea, but also the constant pressure my father felt, the daily struggle to stay afloat; the seemingly ever-present threat of liquidation or closure. So, while this play and its characters are absolutely a work of fiction, the action is rooted in a very specific time and place. In short, I've taken total liberty to both plunder the past and re-invent it.

RC, London, 2017

3

Filthy Business was first performed on 10 March 2017 at Hampstead Theatre, London with the following cast:

ROSA	Babirye Bukilwa
GERARD	Jack Bannon
BERNICE	Callie Cooke
VERN/HARRY	Stephen Critchlow
MONTY	Edmund Derrington
CAROL	Elizabeth Hill
NAT	Louis Hilyer
YETTA	Sara Kestelman
LEO	Dorian Lough
WALTER	Tunji Lucas
EILEEN	Mairead McKinley
TITUS	Keenan Munn-Francis
MICKEY	Callum Woodhouse

Writer	Ryan Craig
Director	Edward Hall
Designer	Ashley Martin-Davis
Lighting	Rick Fisher
Sound	Paul Groothuis
Composer	Simon Slater
Casting	Suzanne Crowley and Gilly Poole

Characters

YETTA SOLOMON

NAT, *her eldest son*

CAROL, *NAT's wife*

BERNICE, *NAT's daughter*

GERARD, *NAT's son*

LEO, *her younger son*

EILEEN, *LEO's wife*

MICKEY, *LEO's son*

MONTY MINSKY, *a machinist*

ROSA, *a machinist*

VERN, *a humper*

WALTER, *ROSA's husband*

HARRY FARRIS, *a loss assessor*

TITUS, *a fourteen-year-old boy*

Time:
*The action takes place over the course of about fourteen years;
from the late 1960s to the early 80s.*

Note:
*The occasional (/) marks the point where the next
speaker interrupts.*

ACT 1

SCENE 1

A rubber shop in North East London. Visible are two storeys of three. The ground level is a showroom with a large counter over which long threads of string hang, coming off balls of string attached to a roof beam. On the counter are order books, a metal spike for receipts, and an ornate, Victorian till machine. Above the counter is a wooden sign that reads; IF IT'S MADE OF RUBBER, WE SELL IT. And next to it is a placard/ sandwich board that reads SPECIALISTS IN RUBBER GOODS OF ALL DESCRIPTIONS that hasn't yet been put out on the pavement. There are other smaller signs with wording on them like; MATTRESSES, PILLOWS, SEATS, CUSHIONS, CARPET UNDERLAY ETC… or PLASTIC FOAM CUSHIONING AND MATS…and in even bigger letters "NO HAGGLING!" and "BROWSERS NOT WELCOME!" To the side of the counter is large butler's sink, with a large black pot, black metal beakers and tea making facilities. Behind the counter are shoddily constructed Dexion shelving units heaving with cushions of varying shapes, sizes and patterns, as well as bits of rubber tubing, matting and piping. In fact there is rubber tubing everywhere, covering the showroom randomly. There is also rubber up and down the staircase which connects all three floors; the unseen basement, the showroom and the top floor which has an office with two desks. NAT, late forties, sits at one of the desks reading a newspaper. A corridor leads off to a kitchenette, toilet and other rooms.

MICKEY, a teenager, sits on the counter swinging his legs. YETTA pounds her fist on the counter as she speaks.

YETTA: I believe in to punish. You got your hand in da till you get it chopped. No discussion.

MICKEY looks blank.

YETTA: Ok not actual chopped, yah, but you see my point. An eyeball for an eyeball, you understand?

MICKEY looks blank.

YETTA: Sure you understand, you're a smart kid. My Leo's kid. You're not no dunce. Some bastard son bitch stole from us and we gotta make him pay. Right?

MICKEY: *(Nothing.)*

YETTA: Bastard son bitch. How could dey do dis? Seventy qvids taken from da till. Now. When we're in *schtuck!* When we're fighting to keep da dogs from da door, *now* dey take from us? Well we gotta fight back boychick. We gotta protect ourselves or we look like chumps, you understand? Sure you understand, you know what's what. (*Closing in on him conspiratorially.*) So. You gonna tell who's da teef?

MICKEY: Me?

YETTA: One of da drivers? One of da *schleppers* was it? One of da stitchers? Who?

MICKEY: I…

YETTA: You don't know?! Sure you don't know. Why would you know? You're a good boy. You don't consort mit t'ieves and *schwindlers*. But, you see, when I find dis bastard son bitch, I'm gonna make him very upset. When dis family gives him a job! Gives him a livelihood! Steal from us?!

MICKEY: *Bubbe…*

YETTA: When we got dem Greeks undercutting us, taking our business. I won't tolerate it you understand? I won't. I half killed myself to build dis place. Yah! Built it from nutting. From grit and blood and scraps of rubber I sold on da streets, and now look. Look at dis place Mickey. Such a shop. Rubber up da stairs, rubber in da basement, rubber in da yard…a temple of rubber….and all of it, one day, all of it yours. Ha? Yours. Waddya tink bout dat when it's at home? *(Notices MICKEY's reticence.)* Hey! Getcha chin off da floor, what's widda face? You don't wanna be a rubber man?

MICKEY: I…

YETTA: Like your *farder*?

MICKEY: Well…

YETTA: Like your Uncle Nat?

MICKEY: I wanna be a ladies' hairdresser.

YETTA: You wanna *what*?

MICKEY: I wanna cut hair…styling and that…

YETTA: Uh huh. Uh huh. *(Smiling strangely.)* Just a moment please. Just one second please. *(Yelling urgently.)* Leo! We got an emergency here! Leo!

MICKEY: Dad's getting the van ready.

YETTA: Nat!

MICKEY: Are you angry?

YETTA: We gotta situation down here! Nat!

NAT: *(From his office.)* Use the tube!

YETTA: What!?

NAT: *(Hardly repressing his frustration.)* Use the speaking tube!

YETTA: *(Picks up the tube and screams into it.)* We gotta situation down here!

MICKEY: *Bubbe* please...

NAT: I'm busy. *(Hangs up the tube.)*

MICKEY: What did I say?

YETTA: *(Spins around to MICKEY furious.)* You wanna hurt me is dat what you want?

MICKEY: I…

YETTA: You wanna kill me down dead?

MICKEY: No.

YETTA: You wan' I should put my face in da cutting machine?

MICKEY: What?

YETTA: *Ladies Hairdresser.* I wanna know where you got such a *fackackta* notion? My own flesh!

MICKEY: I go with Mum sometimes.

YETTA: Oi. Your *Muter.*

MICKEY: I like the colours and that...

YETTA: And what is shampoo? It's *dreck!* Who needs it?

MICKEY: I like the smells...

YETTA: You want *schmell?* Rubber! Dat is da *schmell.*

MICKEY: Rubber reeks. And it's dirty.

YETTA: *Work* is dirty. So what? It's honest.

MICKEY: Aldo says I could make it as a stylist.

YETTA: Aldo!?

MICKEY: Said I had real flare.

YETTA: Some immigrant? What does he know from flare? He'll work you like a mutt and pay you in dirt. No. No. We need you here. We need everyone here. We got troubles *boychick.* We got competitors, *ferocious* competitors.

MICKEY: I could be good at hairdressing, make a real go of it. And it'd only cost a hundred guineas to train. I mean Aldo said it's /worth investing in my future.

YETTA: ...wait a second, wait a second.../wait a minute.

MICKEY: ...if I work a few nights in the salon.../sweeping up, wiping up...

YETTA: *One Undred Guineas?*

MICKEY: What? Yeah. Six months training. It's pretty standard.

YETTA: And where you getting dis *One Undred Gunieas?* Huh? Dipping into our till?

MICKEY: What?

YETTA: Are you da *ganuf*?!

MICKEY: Me!

YETTA: Did you pinch dat money?!

MICKEY: No.

YETTA: Put it towards your crimping? Huh?

MICKEY: I never.

YETTA: Someone's gonna get da sack because of dis boychick? You know dat?

Phone on the counter rings. YETTA glares at MICKEY.

MICKEY: I swear I didn't take that money *Bubbe*. I swear on my life.

YETTA moves towards the phone.

MICKEY: Oh, uh, Dad said not to let you answer the…

YETTA: *(Answers.)* Yah, Sol'mon Rubber, *schpeak*?! What? Do we do cushions? What are you a moron? Yes we do cushions look at dis place. Well if you could see it you'd see it's packed to suffocation mit cushions. *(To MICKEY.)* She's asking do we do cushions… *(To phone.)* What? No I was speaking mit my grandson. He wants to be a hairdresser, whadda ya t'ink of dat one, huh? What about *dat* when it's at home? What? "People always need hairdressers" dat's what you're saying to me? What are you a dunce?

MICKEY: Oh God… *Bubbe*! Stop!

YETTA: *(To MICKEY.)* Don't butt in will ya, I'm doing business here! *(To phone.)* Hello? Now look here you tink we need your money? We got people breaking down da doors for dese cushions. What? Ok. Fuck you up da ass. Huh?

MICKEY: Oh Jesus…

YETTA: I said why don't you go fuck your *muter*, you *dreck*. Now what size cushions you want? What? Rude? So what? You t'ink your five poxy cushions gonna make us rich? Whaddaya outta your rocker? You want poor qvality, sure, go down da street. Go to Thanopoulis. He don't even speak English *propisha.* What? Ok wait wait, I tell you what darlink, since I upset you I do you a deal. A special deal. One moment. *(Covers the receiver and calls upstairs.)* Nat! Nat!

NAT: *(Calling.)* Use the tube! How many times?

YETTA picks up the speaking tube and blows into it.

YETTA: *(Into tube, same volume as before.)* Dunlopillo eight by eights. How much?

NAT: Covered?

YETTA: What?

NAT: Covered?

YETTA: Yah!

NAT: Two and nine-pence apiece.

YETTA: What?

NAT: Two and nine-pence! And you don't /need to yell!

YETTA: *(Hangs up tube and picks up phone.)* Yah hello darlink, yah, yah I just spoke mit my manager and he has aut'orised me to make you a special, one-time-only deal. Just for you darlink. *Four* and nine-pence apiece. Yah. It's a wonderful deal. You'll take 'em? Good for you. And listen, we close at five so don't be after. *(Slams the phone down triumphantly.) Dat* is how you sell a cushion! Write it up in order book.

MICKEY: Me?

YETTA: Come on, come on five latex cushion. You can write can't you, *hairdresser*!?

MICKEY gets an order book and pen. Enter BERNICE, twenty, dressed in a skirt and a too tight shirt to accentuate her impressive bust, she carries a small package wrapped with string.

BERNICE: Oi, you sodding tea leaf. What you done with my grips?

MICKEY: Leave off I ain't touched your grips.

BERNICE: Gimme them grips you little *ganuf!*

YETTA: Hey! Hey! Your cousin says he didn't take no grips.

BERNICE: I *saw* him!

MICKEY: I need 'em for practise.

BERNICE: *(Calling upstairs.)* Dad! Mickey's been at my stuff again!

YETTA: Leave your *farder*, he's a busy man. *(To MICKEY.)* And you, give her back her clips. She needs 'em mit dat monster on her head.

BERNICE: This style's all the rage in Gant's Hill I'll have you know.

YETTA: Whaddya say hairdresser? Tink you can tame dat beast on her *kopf?*

BERNICE: That little *pisher* ain't getting his mitts near my do thanks very much.

MICKEY: Wouldn't wanna touch you anyhow.

YETTA: Hey, hey. Is dat how you talk to a customer? Dey comes in you gotta serve. You gotta smile and be polite. Unless dey're Latvians. Latvians don't buy nutting from nobody. Browsers every last bastard. May dey all choke on der soup and die. *(Spits.)*

BERNICE: *(To MICKEY.)* You didn't let her answer the phone did you?

MICKEY: *(Looks worriedly at YETTA.)* Uhm…

YETTA: Hey Mickey, punch me in da neck! Hard as you like.

MICKEY: Have I got to?

YETTA: Sure you gotta. You gotta be tough in dis life. How you t'ink I survived? I came to dis country, I had to walk half way across Europe to get dat boat. I had nutting. Not even shoes.

BERNICE: What you had bare feet?

YETTA: Don't smart mout' me gerl. I was a child, a little *puppick,* I left everytink I knew, I ran from dat hell hole and never looked back. Got dat boat. Stuffed in da hull, suffocating in dat hull mit da rats. People choking and crying and dying, children screaming like you never heard. And once I'm here, what? Fifteen hour days in dat Whitechapel sweat shop.

BERNICE: We know all that *Bubbe…*

YETTA: You don't know! Pulping rabbit skins in dat basement, you don't know! Making dem coats in da heat and da *schtink…gerls* half your age, miles from home stitching mit so blunt needles and so blistered fingers, half dead in de eyes. Dey would pass out right dere on da floor. Sometimes dead. Bosses did nutting. Stepped over de bodies. We was like animals to dem.

BERNICE: You forgot to tell us how the locals spat at you.

YETTA: Dey did spit! Yah. Dey did spit at us. Said we was taking d'eir jobs. I said "you want to mash rabbits all day for nutting but cold tea and cheese, go ahead." Well. Not me. I swore I'm not gonna rot in dat place, I'm gonna drag myself up. Build sumtink of my own. An Empire! Nobuddy's stepping over my dead body. Now I t'ank God you two don't gotta live like I lived. Cos of dis. Yah? Cos of dis shop!

BERNICE: *(Beat.)* I came to give you these. *(Hands MICKEY the package.)*

MICKEY: Sandwiches? Ace.

BERNICE: Jam and 'all. Mum made 'em for your trip.

YETTA: Yes. Harrogate no less! What an experience for da kid. What a place!

MONTY, twenties, comes up the stairs from the basement. He is intense with a nervous energy, and he is talking almost before he appears.

MONTY: I've had it, I'm telling you now, I've about had it. I simply cannot tolerate it another…. *(Melts on seeing BERNICE.)* Oh…hello Bernice you look nice, I like your hair.

YETTA: Whadda you know from hair? *(To BERNICE.)* You go up and see your farder.

BERNICE goes upstairs.

YETTA: And you stop *kibitzing* and get back to work.

MONTY: I can't work. That's what I'm trying to say, I can't move down there for rubber. I've got to do twenty cushion covers by the end of today, I got no elbow room.

YETTA: Twenty *five*.

MONTY: What?

YETTA: Five more come in just now. /Check order book.

MONTY: *(Looks through the order book.)* Jesus, no, no, no, I got that Bannerman order to get out…

YETTA: *Qvetching*, always *qvetching*…

MONTY: Well it's a health hazard in that basement Mrs. Yetta. Wires poking out every which way, every bit of space stuffed to the gills…I can't even fit in the crapper…

YETTA: So move da stock someplace else. Get Rosa help you. She's tough dat one.

MONTY: I wanna speak to Mr. Leo.

YETTA: He's checking da van.

MICKEY: We're driving to Harrogate.

MONTY: Harrogate? You're getting *more* rubber!

YETTA: You want we should run out?

MONTY: There's matting, there's tubing, there's piping, there's sponge, we're machinists, Mrs. Yetta. Skilled workers…/we need room to manoeuvre…

YETTA: Whaddya want, Nat to move it? Mit his disability?

MONTY: Disability? He lost half a finger. How many years ago? Pre war.

YETTA: You gotta have da full compliment of digits to move dat rubber. / Da full ten.

MONTY: I'm choking down there, do you understand, I'm choking? I'm working with horse hair covers and the fibres...the fibres...they're getting into my lungs, you see, they're taking up residence in my lungs.

YETTA: So charge dem rent. Whaddya want from me?

MONTY: This place is gonna finish me off. I'm telling you. I'm telling you. I'll be sofa stuffing before I'm thirty. Mickey... please...please...I reckon you're the sanest one here, please...tell Mr. Leo...tell him I can't take anymore. Tell him I'm about ready to crack.

YETTA: Put a sock in. All I done for you. You *ingrate*! A little *puppick* you was when I took you in. A child of immigrants who couldn't look after you. And I gave you a home, gave you a family, gave you a trade...gave you a purpose. I brought you up as one of my own, like I gave you life itself. So stop your *qvetching* and get back to work.

MONTY shakes his head and goes back downstairs mumbling to himself.

YETTA: You wanna know what? Dat's your teef.

MICKEY: Monty?

YETTA: He done it. To *schpite* me. I'm telling you. My life. I'll break his fingers.

Enter LEO.

LEO: Van's all set.

MICKEY: Auntie Carol made us sandwiches.

LEO: Lovely, we'll crack 'em open on route.

YETTA: What an adventure you gonna have Mickey. Harrogate.

LEO: You been looking after *Bubbe*?

YETTA: Hey! I can look after myself. Punch me in da neck.

LEO: Maybe later, eh? *(To MICKEY.)* You didn't let her answer the phone did ya?

YETTA: *(Before he can answer.)* Dat *stitcher* was up here. *Qvetching* again.

LEO: Monty?

YETTA: I reckon e's da *ganuf.*

LEO: Don't be daft.

YETTA: *Schpite!* I'm telling you.

LEO: I reckon it's Vern. He's been stirring things with the other drivers.

YETTA: Vern. Dat disloyal *bastard.* You wait till Nat takes care of him.

LEO: *I'll* deal with him. Nat's caused us enough trouble.

YETTA: What trouble?

LEO: *(Reluctantly pulls out a letter and hands it to YETTA.)* Came yesterday.

YETTA: From Garrets. *(Reads in an emotionless monotone.)* "Dear Mr. Solomon, we have been purchasing rubber from your firm for many years and have always been satisfied mit da *qvality* of your goods." Sure, twenty year we supply Garrets. Good customers.

LEO: Keep reading.

YETTA: *(Reading.)* "Two nights ago…your crazy lunatic brother, Nat, barged into our office brandishing a t'ick piece of rubber piping. He grabbed me by da collar and said if I did not cough up da fourteen guineas we owed he'd shove said piping down my t'roat until I started passing latex pellets. Adding "outta my anus." As if I did not get de idea de first time." He don't half paint da picture.

LEO: We were carrying over their fourteen guineas to the next invoice.

YETTA: *(Reading.)* "I have never had any problems dealing mit your tribe before in spite of many warnings…" What da hell he means by "your tribe"?

LEO: Never mind that, get to the end.

YETTA: *(Reading.)* "Suffice it to say, we will not be dealing with your family in da future or, indeed, ever again. Yours sincerely, Reginald Garret." Wow, wow, wow. You wanna know what? I don't t'ink dey're very happy.

LEO: Garrets had ordered ninety mattresses. Nat's seen them off. It's no wonder turnover's down, I'm getting in stock, he's losing buyers.

YETTA: So go 'round dere. Butter dem up. You gotta way about you.

LEO: I tried that, it's too late. They got into bed with the Greeks. Bloody Nat.

YETTA: So whaddya gonna do. Fire him? Your own brother? Where's your loyalty?

LEO: *(Sighs. Notices MICKEY watching him.)*. Mickey go and wait in the van, son.

YETTA: Leave da boy. Let him hear it.

LEO: Mum…

YETTA: It's his family too isn't it?

LEO: We're sinking. We miss the next payment on the lease they close us down.

Pause.

YETTA: Don't worry. Yah. I'll sort it.

LEO: How?

YETTA: Believe me…I been in worse spots.

Enter VERN. A large man in his forties. He heaves a couple sheets of rubber on his back.

VERN: That's the last of it Mr. Leo, I'll stick it in the basement.

LEO: Oh and Vern…come back here when you're done. I wanna to talk to you.

VERN exits to basement. BERNICE comes down the stairs. She sees LEO and smiles flirtatiously.

MICKEY: Are you gonna sack Vern right now, Dad?

LEO: It's wrong to thieve. Hello sweetheart. New hair-do?

YETTA: Why don't you ask it, it's alive?

BERNICE: D'you see I brought sandwiches?

LEO: I did. That's very thoughtful of you Bernie, love.

MICKEY: *She* didn't make them.

BERNICE: I put a bit of string 'round 'em. Don't want 'em leaking on your trousers.

LEO: No. We'll be all right in that department.

BERNICE: Will you bring me back a gift from Harrogate?

LEO: For the girl that has everything?

BERNICE: *(Laughs.)* Don't.

LEO: The guvner gonna join us this morning?

BERNICE: Says he's still busy.

LEO: Yeah. Busy finishing the sports section I shouldn't wonder.

BERNICE: You gonna tell him off?

LEO: Might do, yeah.

BERNICE: Ooh I do like a man who takes charge. See ya. *(She goes.)*

YETTA: You gotta watch dat one.

LEO: She's just a bit lively is all.

YETTA: *(Gesturing upstairs.)* She's like him up dere. Black sheep up dere, reading da sports mit his nine fingers.

VERN returns from the basement.

VERN: Monty gimme lip, but I give him a little shove, told him to shape up.

LEO: …what's all this about you winding up the other drivers.

VERN: What? / Me?

LEO: I can't have agitators in my firm.

VERN: Yeah but we're getting our tyres slashed. Les had a brick thrown at his van…

LEO: Then you come to me.

VERN: You? You're the problem.

LEO: Excuse me?

VERN: Hiring foreigners. What's wrong with an English worker?

YETTA: We give you work don't we.

LEO: Mum…

YETTA: You're English. We had your Beryl here till she got sick. Is it our doing da woman got *varicosed* veins?

LEO: I'll handle this, ok, Mum? Please.

YETTA goes off, muttering.

VERN: Now look Mr, Leo, look, alls I'm saying's if we gotta work with coloureds and whatnot, we deserve a bit extra. Danger money. For the aggro…it's only right.

LEO: You know what I think? I think Rosa should be getting extra to put up with you. You fucking ape. Now get out of my sight, you're sacked.

VERN: Sacked?

LEO: Go on, collect your cards.

VERN: For demanding my rights?

LEO: For 'nicking from the till.

VERN: What? Now wait /a minute I never…

LEO: I don't wanna hear it. Now go on, collect your cards. I'm finished with you.

VERN pushes LEO hard. LEO falls over.

MICKEY: Dad!

LEO: *(Getting up.)* I'm all right…

VERN: I'm talking to Mr. Nat. *(He heads upstairs.)*

LEO: I'm gonna wash up. Then we'll set off. *(Exits to the back office.)*

NAT exits his office holding a package and meets VERN on the stairs.

VERN: This is a grave error Mr. Nat. A grave error. Man and boy I worked for this family and he treats me like dirt.

NAT: Who does?

VERN: And that blackie just got off the boat. I need this job Mr. Nat. My Beryl's got terrible veins.

NAT: What are you blathering on about?

VERN: Mr. Leo. He gave me the boot. Says I thieved money.

NAT: Ignore Leo.

VERN: What? Ignore him…but…he's…

NAT: I'm senior to him.

VERN: Yeah, but…

NAT: *(Menacing.)* But what?

VERN: Nothing, nothing, /no, I just…

NAT: Good. Now stop snivelling and get back to work.

VERN: Oh thank you, thank you, no, no, I really appreciate this Mr. Nat. /I do…

NAT: Long as you remember who's buttering your bread. *(VERN looks blank.)* Eyes and ears Vern, that's what I need. Eyes and ears. Understand?

VERN: Y-you need something doing you just gimme the nod, I'm your man. *(Goes.)*

NAT goes to the counter. With a Stanley knife he cuts off a length of string from one of the strands hanging down and tries to tie the package. It's fiddly work with no index finger.

MICKEY: *(Watches NAT struggle. Finally…)* Can I help? Dad showed me how.

NAT looks at MICKEY for a beat, then hands him the package and string. MICKEY swiftly and expertly ties the package. NAT watches, beadily.

NAT: Off to Harrogate today are you? With your old dad?

MICKEY: Yeah.

NAT: *Bubbe* tell you it was a dream of a place did she?

MICKEY: Yeah. Aunty Carol made us sandwiches.

NAT: Oh yeah? What's in 'em?

MICKEY: Jam.

NAT: Jam eh? *(NAT smiles at MICKEY, but it's loaded with threat. Pause.)* Your Dad ever tell you how I lost my finger?

MICKEY: *(Shakes his head.)* No.

NAT: *(Puts his arm around MICKEY's shoulder.)* We had a stall in Leather Lane. Market there. Trade was brisk so Thanapolus and his boy wanted a piece of the action. Horned in our turf. I thought I'm not having that…I got myself a nice length of tubing…smashed their stall up. Upended it, had the old bubble on the ground…thumb in the wind pipe. His boy only had a shotgun. Took a pot shot at me the little tyke. Blew my digit clean off. Nasty, ton of blood, but I tell you what? No-one ever took Nat Solomon for a chump after that. *(Puts a good finger on MICKEY's head and presses hard.)* So just you remember that sunshine. Ok?

NAT goes upstairs, passing LEO coming down, cleaned up. MICKEY avoids LEO's glance.

LEO: Eight thirty. We should've hit the tarmac by now?

GERARD enters. He is seventeen, a bit slow, stands to attention as he tries, haltingly to speak.

LEO: All right there Gerard? Did you wanna say something son?

GERARD: *(Almost as if rehearsed.)* Hello. Please. Uncle Leo, please can…please can I come on the trip with you. And Mickey? I could help out. Help. Hump.

LEO: I don't mind son, but you got to ask your Old Man. *(GERARD runs upstairs to the office.)* Mickey come on, look lively. You got them jam sarnies?

GERARD: Dad! Can I go? With Uncle Leo. And Mickey?

NAT: No you bloody can't. *(GERARD, crestfallen, slopes out to the balcony.)*

LEO: Well kiddo, what's the verdict?

GERARD: Dad said I couldn't go!

LEO: Never mind. Another time eh son? Right then Nat, we're off! *(They go.)*

NAT: *(From office.)* For Gawd's sake drive careful! That rubber cost money!

SCENE 2

That night. A council flat in Well's Road, Hackney. Rolls of rubber sheeting lean against the walls and sideboard, and uncovered Dunlopillo cushions are stacked in corners.

CAROL, NAT's nervous, eager-to-please wife looks out the window. On the table are four uneaten plates and one finished plate. NAT sits in a large armchair reading a newspaper. EILEEN, forties, fiery temper, Belfast accent, sits staring at NAT, struggling to contain her fury.

CAROL: You know what this puts me in mind of. The war. We'd sit together. Waiting for news. Wouldn't we Nelly? Waiting for news of Leo. Out there. All over he went, didn't he Nat? Normandy, Africa…The Levant. Right in the thick of it he was.

NAT reads the paper, shifts, irritated, in his seat. EILEEN picks up on NAT's ire.

EILEEN: I'll clear these plates…

CAROL: It's all right love /I'll do it.

EILEEN: Stay where you are love, I can manage. *(Exits with the full plates of food.)*

NAT: She's been giving me the skunk eye all night.

CAROL: I'm sure she's just anxious about the boys.

NAT: *(Back to his paper.)* Hmm.

CAROL: You can't blame her, poor love. Shocking weather. And them roads can be treacherous, you said it yourself. Van loaded up. You think they've had an accident?

NAT: How the bleeding hell should I know?

CAROL: Black ice. And those vans are none too clever. Oh God, they could be in a hospital somewhere. God knows where. *Sheffield.* They could be in a hospital in *Sheffield.*

NAT: Keep your voice down for /crying out loud.

CAROL: I never thought it was sensible driving all that way in one go.

NAT: It's cheaper.

CAROL: Eileen looks ashen. The haddock's ruined.

NAT: I told you both to eat, no sense in wasting /good grub.

CAROL: Thank God you didn't let Gerard go with them, that's all I can think. He was so keen to be with Mickey, bless him. Thank God it's *them* out there and not you two.

NAT: I beg your pardon? You think *I'd* do that journey. Do I look like a chump?

Enter EILEEN just about containing her anxiety and fury.

CAROL: Oh…love…we was just saying, weren't we Nat…we… we was just saying we're quite sure they're all right. Leo's done that journey hundreds of times. Hasn't he Nat?

NAT: Thousands.

CAROL: Thousands. Up and down, up and down….

EILEEN: *(Under her breath.)* And whose fault's that?

NAT: Excuse me? /You say something Nelly?

CAROL: Oh yes we were just saying it's probably just traffic. Weren't we Nat? There's always a lot of traffic if it's bad weather or if there's been an accident or…

NAT: Carol /for Gawd's sake…

CAROL: Oh God I didn't mean they'd been in an accident. Ooh I'm so stupid sometimes. I'm such an idiot. Useless. Useless.

NAT: I don't know why you gotta fill every bleeding silence.

CAROL: I can't help it, it's my nature. I don't mean no harm, love, just trying to help.

EILEEN: Maybe you should go home. I'll call if I need anything.

CAROL: Oh no we couldn't leave you. Not like this. Could we Nat?

NAT: I'm going nowhere till I see that rubber's back in one piece.

CAROL: That's the ticket. Family sticks together.

Awkward beat. EILEEN sits. Seethes.

NAT: If he weren't so bloody pig headed.

EILEEN: Excuse me?

NAT: You know he insists on taking them back doubles. The "scenic route" he calls it. I tell him not to but he's stubborn.

EILEEN: Oh so this is all Leo's fault?

NAT: Keep to the main roads I tell him, you can't go wrong on the main roads.

CAROL: That's true, I've heard him say that...

NAT: I just hope that rubber gets back in one piece. That's all I hope.

EILEEN: Oh as long as the rubber's back safe.

NAT: What d'you think pays for that frock you're wearing?

CAROL: Nat please...

NAT: What'd'ya think pays for this flat? Rubber. So don't go shooting me dirty looks.

CAROL: That's enough Nat.../please...

NAT: You think anyone'd pay us if not for me? They wouldn't cough up for Leo. They think he's a mug!

EILEEN: You will not talk about him like that in this house!

CAROL: Stop it now, Nelly knows you work yourself silly in that shop, don't you?

EILEEN: Do I?

NAT: You wanna know the truth? He's buggered without me!

EILEEN: Well we'll soon see about that won't we!

EILEEN kicks herself. NAT smells blood and stands.

EILEEN: Look, maybe you should go home. I'll have him call when he gets in?

CAROL: Good idea.

NAT: I wanna know what you mean by that remark. "We'll see about that"?

EILEEN: It means nothing.

CAROL: Nat…

NAT: What's going on Nelly?

EILEEN: Maybe he's tired of being taken for granted.

NAT: Tired?

CAROL: Oh now.

NAT: Tired of his own family?

EILEEN: Can you blame him? That shop's nothing without him. His talents. His way with the punters. His gift for fixing things up. Meanwhile you got him schlepping up and down the country fetching rubber you don't need.

NAT: Don't need?

EILEEN: I see the books Nat, you're over stocking. That's why the place is sinking.

NAT: Why's Leo off to Harrogate to get more then?

EILEEN: Because the idiot doesn't want to show you up. Outta some twisted sense of bloody loyalty God help us.

NAT: You're out of your depth Nelly. All right? /Watch your mouth.

CAROL: Nat's right dear, us women don't understand about business…

EILEEN: Carol will you do me a favour and please *shut up?*

NAT: Here, here.

Then a noise outside. EILEEN runs to the window.

EILEEN: It's them. Thank God. *(She runs into the hall.)*

LEO: *(Outside.)* Hello, hello, the wanderers return.

EILEEN: *(Outside.)* Look at you two.

LEO: *(Outside.)* Engine packed up. Middle of a bloody cyclone.

EILEEN: *(Outside.)* For Heaven's sake.

LEO and MICKEY (in a dark mood) enter, covered in dust and oil, followed by EILEEN, who immediately goes to the side table to pour LEO a whisky.

LEO: The voyagers return.

CAROL: Thank Heavens

NAT: How's that rubber?

LEO: Fine.

NAT: Thank Gawd for that.

CAROL: I knew that van was on the blink.

LEO: Royal Engineers wasn't I, I can fix a tank, you think I can't handle a Bedford?

EILEEN: *(Bringing LEO the whisky.)* I've been going out of my mind.

LEO: Had them jam sandwiches of yours Carol. Saved our skins didn't they son?

MICKEY: Can I go to my room now?

EILEEN: No, Jam Sandwiches isn't a proper tea, I'll make you eggs. Wash up.

MICKEY goes to the bathroom. LEO goes to top up his whisky. EILEEN goes into the kitchen.

LEO: How's trade?

NAT: Slow.

LEO: Monty finish that Bannerman order?

NAT: Staying late. Rosa too.

LEO: She's a good girl that one. Loyal.

NAT: I'm not paying her any overtime if that's her game.

LEO: Nah. She wants to do well is all, she's a nice little worker…

NAT: Oh and I hired Vern back. That all right?

LEO: You did what?

NAT: Well, he seemed a bit miffed.

LEO: He thieved Nat.

NAT: He was begging me, what could I do?

LEO: You know he gave me a shove. Knocked me over. In front of the boy.

NAT: You're overreacting. Don't you think he's overreacting Carol?

CAROL: His wife does have terrible varicose veins Leo.

LEO: Thing is Carol love, there's a code. He put his hand on me. How's it look; I sack a feller one minute, you hire 'em back the next?

NAT: What do you care? From what I hear, you're half way out the door.

A sudden, cold silence. LEO glares at NAT.

NAT: That's what your old woman says anyway. She lying or what?

Beat. LEO goes to the side table and pours himself a whisky.

CAROL: Don't let's have bad blood eh Nat, we've had such a lovely evening.

NAT: Lovely evening? Nelly's barely spoke to you all night. Shooting me dirty looks, meanwhile we're all sitting there not mentioning the real issue.

LEO: Which is what?

CAROL: Let's go home now eh Nat.

NAT: …makes me laugh he does.

LEO: Which is what Nat?

CAROL: Come on, /it's been a long night.

NAT: Which is you're jumping ship while your kid's on the fiddle.

LEO: What?

CAROL: Oh /Nat, no…

LEO: What did you say?!

NAT: Mickey's the one who pinched that seventy quid, not Vern.

LEO: You're fingering my boy?

NAT: You're always showing him that sodding till. /So proud of it…

LEO: You're calling my son a thief?

NAT: Opportunity, know-how, motive. /He had all three.

LEO: What motive?

CAROL: Leave it now love.

NAT: The man should know what's going on in his own house. Your son wants to be a hairdresser.

LEO: …he what…?

NAT: He's been working on the sly for some wop. Stole the money for training.

LEO: Rubbish.

NAT: Ask Bernice. Poor cow can't track down her fucking hair grips. She's livid.

EILEEN comes in with two plates of eggs that she sets down on the table. MICKEY enters.

LEO: What's your game here Nat? I wanna know. /What're you up to?

NAT: Oh come on Leo, anyone can see he's bent as a nine-bob note.

LEO: *(Squaring up to NAT.)* Say that again.

NAT: A tea leaf and a queer! That's what you raised!

LEO slaps NAT in the face. Gasps. Silence. NAT glares at LEO.

NAT: Big hero.

LEO: Go on. Clear off.

NAT: Yeah. That's loyalty for you, eh Carol. Waste of air, the lot of you.

NAT goes, CAROL follows. EILEEN approaches LEO and touches his face. LEO pushes her away and turns to MICKEY.

LEO: I want you to cut it out with this hairdressing caper.

MICKEY: And do what? Be like you? Get played for a chump.

LEO: What did you say? You want me to take my belt to you boy!?

EILEEN: That's enough both of you. Leo wash up for tea. Mickey eat your eggs.

LEO goes. MICKEY sits grumpily at the table and eats his food. EILEEN wacthes him.

EILEEN: I wanna tell you about when your father and I met.

MICKEY: Oh Jesus. I'm not really in the mood for the romance of the century.

EILEEN: Shut up and listen. Belfast. 1941. I was working in the NAAFE for the British Army. Your Dad was already the most decorated soldier in the unit. And so bloody handsome it made you want to scream. All the girls loved him, but it was me he had eyes for.

MICKEY: ...and he'd sneak out of barracks to see you, I heard it a million times...

EILEEN: ...but what you don't know is that one night he was kidnapped. *(Off MICKEY's disbelieving look.)* As God is my witness. We lived on the Falls Road and that bloody fool's wandering about in his British Army uniform. He could've been court martialled if the RA didn't shoot him first. One night he's coming to meet me this gang jumps him. Chuck him in the back of a truck, sack over his head, they drive him deep into the woods. When they get there they take off the sack and he sees them. *(LEO enters holding his jacket and hangs back.)* My own brothers. Four of the maniacs anyway. They shove a gun in his face and say "You keep away from our sister or we'll kneecap you. And we'll piss on you while you scream." Then that father of yours, you know what he says? He says "I'm not staying away from her, so go on, do your worst. It makes no difference cos I love her and I'm gonna marry her and neither you nor the Republicans nor the British Bloody Army are gonna stop me." Well. Tears…tears came into their eyes. They put down their guns and clasped your father to their breasts, kissing him and telling him he was their brother now. Weeping and hugging each other and declaring that our wedding will be the greatest event Belfast has ever seen. Meanwhile nobody asked me what I thought of marrying this suicidal imbecile and moving to Hackney for the rest of my bloody life. Point is your father is not a chump. He's just got a weakness when it comes to his family. Like a lot of fighting men. Now off to bed with you.

MICKEY goes. EILEEN clears plates and almost jumps on seeing LEO standing by the entrance.

LEO: What you telling him about all that for? *(Puts on his jacket.)*

EILEEN: Where're you going?

LEO: I wanna check on that Bannerman order.

EILEEN: What about your eggs?

LEO: Don't stay up. *(Goes to the door.)*

EILEEN: When are you gonna tell them Leo?

LEO: *(Stops at the door.)* Soon. I just…I gotta wait until things settle.

EILEEN: When do things ever *settle* in that madhouse?

LEO: Nelly…

EILEEN: You're too soft. You let them muck you about because they're family, and you can't you see how little they respect you.

LEO: Christ I said I'd buy the place didn't I?! / I said so didn't I?

EILEEN: You made me a promise to me. /To tell them you'd leave.

LEO: And what about your promise to keep schtum, eh? / Couldn't do it, could you?

EILEEN: …yes because…yes /because I'm…

LEO: No, you had to drop little hints to Nat. When I told you…/when I asked you…

EILEEN: Because I'm scared Leo! I heard about the attacks. On toppa everything else. My God, one day someone's gonna get killed in that bloody shop.

LEO: I'm going.

EILEEN: You've never been like this with me! Cold. Never.

There is a pregnant moment between them. LEO comes over, touches her chin.

LEO: Chin up.

LEO goes. EILEEN is frozen to the spot.

SCENE 3

The shop. WALTER, a smartly dressed Nigerian man in his twenties, bangs on the locked front door. MONTY enters from the basement.

WALTER: *(From outside.)* Hello! Shop!

MONTY: We're closed. /Sorry.

WALTER: *(From outside.)* I am here to talk to Rosa.

MONTY: Rosa?

MONTY opens the door. WALTER barges past him, removes his hat.

WALTER: I am in the right place. Solomon Rubber.

MONTY: Yeah but…

WALTER: I want to see Rosa. Bring her come please.

MONTY: Rosa's busy at the minute.

WALTER: Rosa! Come out here will you please?!

MONTY: Now wait a minute, you can't just waltz in /and start hollering…

WALTER: I am finished with you now. Go away. Rosa!

MONTY: Right. I'll have to ask you to leave.

WALTER pulls out a knife.

WALTER: Stay back. You hear what I said? You hear what I said!

MONTY: I heard you, Jesus…

WALTER: Rosa! Get out here woman!

YETTA enters.

YETTA: Hey! What's all da yelling?

WALTER: Stay where you are old woman. I want Rosa.

YETTA: Rosa got work to finish.

WALTER: Shut up. And do not move from that spot unless you want to be cut.

YETTA: Dis is my shop. I don't have no funny business in my shop!

WALTER: I will speak to my wife! You hear me!

MONTY: Wife?

WALTER: *(Spins round to threaten MONTY.)* You! I said stay
where you are!

*While WALTER has his back to her, YETTA grabs a length of rubber
tubing and whacks him over the head. WALTER is stunned and drops
the knife to grab his head.*

YETTA: Get it!

MONTY runs to pick up the knife and gives it to YETTA.

YETTA: OK. Now get back to work. Go.

MONTY: And leave you with him?

YETTA: I take care of myself. Get back down der before I bash
you too.

*MONTY goes down to the basement. WALTER groans and tries to
pick himself up.*

YETTA: Let me tell you somet'ing mister; when dem bastard
Kossacks came to my village I fought back. Dey burned
every damn t'ing in da place, beat people, shot dem, used
my sister how dey want, used my *muter.* Not me. I hit.
I scratched. I bit. I went for da t'roat. I was ten. Dey set
dogs on us. I barked back. I barked louder. We was lice
to dem. Not here. Not in dis shop. Dis shop is *my* country.
Nobuddy fucks mit me in dis shop.

Pause. WALTER starts laughing.

YETTA: Sum'ting funny?

WALTER: Actually yes, you remind me of my mother.

YETTA: Really? Well she'd be ashamed. Pulling a knife on a
defenceless old woman.

WALTER: Defenceless! Ha! *(Checks his head.)*

YETTA: What is it, you bleeding?

WALTER: Forget it.

YETTA: You need bandage? What's a matter? I get you
bandage.

WALTER: I said stop fussing woman. Why you women always fuss? I carry for protection OK? Four of them the other night. Jumped me. Called me jungle bunny, politely requested I return home. I said that is where I am going, I live on the Balls Pond Road.

YETTA: She never said nutting about no husband.

WALTER: Back home I was an important man. A journalist. For sports. Try getting a job as a sports writer in England looking like this.

YETTA: Yah yah I don't want to hear no sob story shit from you. You want to talk suffering mit me? My people got five t'ousand years of suffering. Beat dat.

WALTER: Oh you think we are the same you and I? We are not the same. Do you have little kids grabbing at your skin, they wanna see if the paint comes off? Do you have that?

YETTA: No.

WALTER: No. The British. Please. All that talk of fair play, all that nonsense about cricket. They drew our borders, raped our country, then they expect us to take responsibility for the mess.

YETTA: Listen mister I got my own problems.

WALTER: Promises were made! They said we would be welcomed here. With open arms. So why am I spat at in the street? Beaten? Rejected? Abused by the police? Why do they hate the African? The indignities I have to endure every day in this city. If I knew what was ahead of me I would have stayed in Nigeria to be hacked to pieces by the fanatics.

YETTA: People used to check my head for horns: said we was devils, said we killed Jesus. I said I done some t'ings in my time missus but don't go fingering me for dat one.

WALTER: You had the same choice as me. Stay and die or leave and face scorn.

YETTA: Wait, you tink we are da same? We is not da same. I don't go about t'reatening my own people. You say Rosa's your wife.

WALTER: She *is* my wife.

YETTA: Ok so you gotta protect her. When you got no nation, no government, no place in da world what *do* you got? Family. Dat's what? You can't depend on nutting else.

WALTER: I did not come here to trade miseries I want to see my wife. Bring her come.

YETTA: I said she's working.

WALTER: I am growing tired of this…

YETTA: Rosa is *my* family now. She is my people. She got fire in her eye dat one, I see it. She came here mit nutting, wants to pull herself up…mit hard work. So. Now she got me looking out for her. I protect her like a mama tarantula. Loyalty is everyt'ing to me.

WALTER steps back, smiles.

WALTER: Ok then, if she's your people, you owe me too.

YETTA: I?

WALTER: Her debt is your debt. Seventy English Pounds.

YETTA: What? What did you say?

WALTER: Does she not understand? It cost money to get her here. The boatman must be paid. I must be paid. I need to live too. I cannot work. They will not let me work.

YETTA: My Rosa owes you seventy qvids, dat's what you telling me?

WALTER: I arranged the transportation, the papers, I made her legal and it cost me. But these men are not playing. If they come here, they will not be as amenable as I, believe me.

YETTA: And she agreed to pay you dis moneys?

WALTER: By today. Yes. Now I am not a violent man, but if I am pushed...

YETTA goes to the till. Takes out money and counts out seventy pounds.

YETTA: Here. Take it. Den stay away from Rosa.

WALTER looks at the money. Then, with as much dignity as possible, takes the money.

WALTER: You were serious about that loyalty thing then? *(He laughs ruefully and exits.)*

YETTA picks up the speaking tube.

YETTA: Monty, send Rosa up here. *Qvick.*

YETTA paces. ROSA appears from the basement.

YETTA: Some character come here just now...says he's your husband.

ROSA looks down.

YETTA: Look at me.

ROSA looks up, locks eyes with YETTA.

YETTA: Dis is correct? Huh?

ROSA: Yes.

YETTA: Says you owe him money.

ROSA: I'm sorry Mrs. Yetta but that is my own business.

YETTA: Some *meshugga's* waving a blade in my showroom, now it's my business.

ROSA: He did what?

YETTA: You lied to me.

ROSA: I...

YETTA: You said your papers was kosher.

ROSA: I...I had to work.

YETTA: You made me into a criminal, I can't employ illegals, dey close me down.

ROSA: Please don't report me. They will send me back. /I cannot go back.

YETTA: I *should* report you.

ROSA: I will work harder. I'll work weekends for free. Whatever /you need.

YETTA: I can't risk it.

ROSA: I did not mean to lie to you. Please.

YETTA: Doesn't matter you lied. You stole.

ROSA: Stole?!

YETTA: I t'ought you was loyal. I saw myself in you.

ROSA: I would never steal from you. I would cut off my own arm first…

MONTY enters form the basement in his coat, watches this….

YETTA: You knew he was coming here tonight? Dis *husband.*

ROSA: I…

YETTA: You knew he's owed seventy *qvid,* you promised to pay him?

ROSA: …yes but…

YETTA: Suddenly seventy *qvid* goes missing from da till. It's a coincidence?! You tink I'm soft in da nut? Who else would take it? Who else would betray me like dis?

ROSA: *(Realising. To herself.)* Oh God…Oh /my God…

YETTA: Huh? Who? Tell me, I'll flay dem alive.

ROSA: *(Beat. Lying.)* I do not know.

YETTA: You shoulda come to me. You got trouble you come to me. Why didn't you come to me? Huh? You hurt me Rosa. *(Notices MONTY.)* You people tink I don't got no feelings?

(Goes to the till, opens it.) You made trouble for a lotta people today *gerl.* Here.

ROSA: Mrs. Yetta…

YETTA: Twenty pounds, take it. Nobuddy says Yetta Solomon don't play fair. Take it.

ROSA: I cannot.

YETTA: And don't worry, I took care of your *meshugga* husband. He won't bodder you no more. *(She offers the twenty again.)* Go on. Take it.

ROSA: I cannot take that money.

YETTA: You wanna starve? Take it. Buy a little machine. You're a good seamstress. Work hard, work all hours. Work will save you. Take it. *(ROSA takes money.)*. Ok, now get your coat and go. *(ROSA goes. YETTA turns to MONTY.)* Bannerman order done?

MONTY: What? Oh. Yes. All done.

YETTA: OK. When she's gone, lock up. *(Notices MONTY wants to speak.)*

You got sumtink to say to me?

MONTY: *(Pause. Glares at YETTA. Finally…)* No. Nothing.

YETTA goes. MONTY rubs his face from exhaustion. LEO appears.

LEO: All right Monty son, it's late. I'm gonna cash up, you go home.

MONTY: Mr Leo…

LEO: Go on, 'fore I change my mind.

MONTY goes. LEO starts to shut off the lights. ROSA comes up in her coat, startled to see LEO.

LEO: *(Grins.)* There she is. *(ROSA's not amused.)* I got something for you. Present. *(Pulls money from his pocket.)* Seventy quid. That's how much you needed wasn't it?

ROSA: *(Quietly.)* I knew it was you.

LEO: Yeah. I'm quite something aren't I? Happy?

ROSA: I never asked you to do this.

LEO: Look just take it. Get Walter off your back, pay off your debt.

ROSA: Do you know what you've done? You bloody fool.

LEO: …look love I'm still your boss…

ROSA: No you are not. You are not my boss anymore?!

LEO: What?

ROSA: I'm dismissed. Because of your stupid bloody-minded meddling in my affairs.

LEO: …wait a minute, hold up…

ROSA: He was here. You bloody idiot. Walter was here. Waving a knife!

LEO: Here?!

ROSA: Shouting how I owed him *seventy* pounds.

LEO: I'll fix this. I will /fix this.

ROSA: Please don't. Don't fix any more.

LEO: Rosy. *(He takes her arm, stops her from going.)*

ROSA: I respectfully ask that you not interfere further in my affairs.

LEO: *(Touches her face.)* I'm gonna leave all this, leave Nelly.

ROSA: No!

LEO: Leave it all, everything that's being pinning me down, / pressing me down.

ROSA: I never asked you to do that.

LEO: I got ideas Rosy. Lots of ideas. Come with me. I'll need a decent machinist.

ROSA: Please let me go….

LEO: But I think it could be better with you. I could be a better man with you.

ROSA: Stop! *(Finally finding the strength to pull away.)* Stop. *(Sees LEO looking at her forlornly. She softens.)* Just stop. *(ROSA exits.)*

LEO ponders a moment, then goes to the till machine and empties all the cash into a money case. He then carefully places a heavy protective covering over the machine and disappears down to the basement to switch off the rest of the power.

Enter THREE MEN in balaclavas and holding crow bars. FIRST MAN gestures for a second balaclava-ed man to hang about by the corridor as look-out as the others grab the money case and smash it open with the crow bar, taking all the money. LEO returns and sees FIRST MAN and the third balaclava-ed man.

LEO: Oi! No you don't!

The intruders are caught off guard. LEO wrestles the bar off the FIRST MAN and whacks the THIRD in the groin. The SECOND MAN on look-out strikes LEO violently over the head. LEO drops to the floor and the MEN kick him savagely. They smash up the shelving units, douse the shop with petrol. As they leave they light a Molotov cocktail and lob it down into the basement and exit.

Act II

SCENE 1

Three days later. Lights up on the Shop. The charred remains. A massive fire has all but destroyed the whole premises. Newly daubed across the walls are the words: "Scum. Yids Go Home" and a swastika. A man in a sombre suit and hat, FARRIS, is standing in the dim light making notes in a small book. NAT and GERARD appear outside.

NAT: *(Off.)* Clear off you little pricks. Fuck off!

> *The man darts out of sight. GERARD enters and looks around at the damage. Enter NAT.*

NAT: Wait outside. Watch those little bastards don't get back in.

> *GERARD goes. NAT goes upstairs. YETTA enters and inspects the daubing.*

YETTA: Wow, wow, wow will ya look at dis.

NAT: *(Coming back down. About the daubing.)* That was local kids. They musta snuck in past the cordon.

YETTA: Dey shouldn'ta done dis. Not dis.

NAT: They're just kids, they don't know any better.

YETTA: But look. Look at dis filt'. It's not enough we get burned, we gotta get vandalised too?

NAT: Fire chief said not to touch nothing till they finish the investigation.

YETTA: What? Dey make us wait t'ree days to get in and we can't touch?

NAT: It's protocol.

YETTA: Protocol, crap. Protocol didn't stop dem little Nazis breaking in and putting up dis filt'.

NAT: All we need's a good loss assessor, we'll be fine.

YETTA: Loss assessors? Hyenas do lot of 'em. Da *dreck* of society.

NAT: They're beating down the door. Got here before the fire brigade, some of 'em.

YETTA: Rubber burns, dis game you live mit da danger. But dis…look what dese little bastards done.

NAT: Thank God we still got all the stock Leo picked up.

YETTA: What do I tell you, always have stock. Stock is life. It's a God Blessing.

NAT: Everything else is ruined. Materials, machines, paperwork, all of it.

YETTA: *(Goes to till machine which is covered and still in one piece.)* Not all of it.

NAT: *(Joins her at the till.)* Bloody Leo. Cares for it like a pet.

YETTA: Leo, Leo, Leo… What in hell was he doing here dat night? He's was meant ot be on da road.

NAT: *Schtupping* the new girl.

YETTA: *(Looks at him, horrified.)* Rosa?!

NAT: I reckon he was planning to take her with him when he left.

YETTA: What? *(She almost gasps for breath.)* Left?!

NAT: I asked around. He's been making enquiries about a warehouse, Western Road way.

NAT yanks the protective cover away to reveal a glittering, perfectly preserved till machine.

YETTA: Never. Not my Leo. Turn his back on his people. Never.

NAT: This as an opportunity. A chance to put things in the proper order. Once it's all made official that I'm in charge…

YETTA: What? You?

NAT: I'm the eldest. It's only right.

YETTA: What do you know from right?

NAT: We're under attack. From all sides. Now I've shown you I can handle things. That I don't tolerate liberty takers. We need a strong arm at the helm now. Someone who'll crack heads to put this place back together. I'll terrify them Greeks, I'll do whatever it takes.

YETTA: I don't wanna talk about it.

As they talk a man enters in an ill-fitting suit, FARRIS. He is unseen by NAT or YETTA.

NAT: I've shown you I'm loyal. Ma. Haven't I? Time and again. Leo's not.

YETTA: My poor Leo.

NAT: You gotta tell him. Tell him who's running things from now on.

FARRIS: Would you believe it? Not a scratch.

NAT and YETTA spin round to see HARRY FARRIS, a man in his forties with an inclination to be florid with his language.

FARRIS: A survivor. May I?

YETTA and NAT look at each other, bemused.

FARRIS: *(He goes to the till and examines it.)* If I'm not mistaken… a National Sixty Three Combination Mechanism Till, Late Victorian era. Clam Shell inlay? *(He opens it, gasps.)* Lily of the Valley. Of course. It really is a beautiful object. A work of art almost.

YETTA: T'anks. Now fuck away. We busy.

FARRIS: Oh. /No, I…

YETTA: No customers today. Can't you see we got issues?

FARRIS: Sorry no, the name's Farris. Harry Farris. Farris and Farris Loss Assessors. *(Proffers a business card.)*

NAT: Another fire engine chaser.

FARRIS: Nineteen apparently.

NAT: What?

FARRIS: Fire engines. That's how many it took to put out the fire. It was a major conflagration. Had to evacuate the entire street, close off the roads for miles around...

YETTA: What kind of idiot name is Harry Farris? I don't trust men mit sing-song names.

FARRIS: *(Examining the damage.)* Well trust is absolutely key madam and I think if you hear me out, you'll be keen to engage my services.

NAT: Go on then. Make your pitch.

FARRIS: Thank you. If you'd allow me a moment to do my work.

FARRIS walks about examining the damage. He sees the graffiti, and tuts, shaking his head.

FARRIS: Dear oh dear oh dear. Will you look at this? This... this is not my England. No sir, not the England I was brought up to believe in. The England of quiet decency, of tolerance. The England my father gave a lower limb to help preserve. *(Pulls a pencil from his jacket and chips off some of the charred wall.)* ...Fought alongside men of every race and creed he did. Africans, West Indians, Poles, Ghurkas. Sikhs. Side by side they fought...in the spirit of Wellington and Marlborough, of Blake and Kipling. Of Brooke.

YETTA: *(Aside to NAT.)* Da man is an emotional mental case. Get him outta here.

FARRIS: If I should die think only this of me...that there's some corner of a foreign field that is forever England. *(Looks directly at YETTA.)* There shall be in that rich earth, a richer dust concealed. It was you who started the firm was it madam?

YETTA: What? Oh. Sure. Sure. Built dis place outta nutting! Worked like a dog all my days. Nobuddy retailed rubber before me. I invented da whole concept.

FARRIS: It's all good. Adds a strong emotional charge to the claim, a great narrative.

YETTA: Narrative! It's not a narrative, it's my life. My Zikkel was a big man. A *schtarker*. And tough. Dey put him to work in dis stinking tram factory, working da wheels. Cutting great hunks of rubber into shape and fixing dem on. Terrible work. Dangerous. Sliced his hands to bloody ribbons day after day. One night he brings home a bag. It's full of off-cuts. He said dey was going to t'row it away. Good rubber. It's a waste. I says waddya want me to do mit it. He says you make tings. Make somtink. So. I gotta knife…started cutting up dem bits of rubber. Making tings, fashioning tings. Soles for shoes, bottle stoppers, washers for taps… all night I worked. Sunday morning, first ting, I go down Leather Lane …sold 'em on da market. Penny each item. Cleared out of stock in t'ree hours. Gave people what dey want. What dey need. I told my husband you keep bringing home scraps I turn dem into gold. Year after year we sell, more and more, we get bigger and bigger, more stalls, more items, den…dis place. Dis shop. All outta bits of rubber dey was t'rowing away. I built an empire outta dem scraps.

FARRIS: May I tell you what I'm hearing? I'm hearing the story of how this city was built. From people like you. People with grit and invention…people who create opportunity…who forge their paths. That's why these immigrant firms are the beating heart of our economy.

YETTA: Hey. Who you calling immigrant? You little *pisher*. I'm as British as you are, I sweat blood for dis country.

FARRIS: That's exactly what I'm talking about. The sacrifice… the hours and hours of labour…the family pulling together in the great human quest for a better life.

NAT scoffs under his breath.

FARRIS: Plus you've found a market, you've created jobs...
and I can use that. Once the investigation into the cause
of the fire's completed I can start lobbying the insurance
company on your behalf. I can top any of my competitors
by fifteen percent.

NAT: You seem pretty sure of yourself.

FARRIS: Ask around Mr. Solomon, my record speaks for
itself. Call me when you decide. *(Goes to leave and turns on
a thought.)* Oh by the way, that antique cash machine...
just as a matter of interest...if that hadn't been preserved
so diligently it'd fetch a hefty sum. Til I've taken the
inventory, I've seen nothing...officially speaking. You learn
fast not to be sentimental in my line of work. *(FARRIS exits.)*

NAT: I don't think I've met an oilier little chancer in all my life.

YETTA: Exactly. Hire him. Soon as possible.

NAT: You didn't swallow that crap?

YETTA: Not a word, but who could argue mit dat lunatic? He'll
talk your head off.

NAT: Fine. I'll call him in the morning.

YETTA: And burn dat till. You heard da man. No room for
sentiment in business. And batter it up before you do.
Make it look real.

*YETTA goes. NAT puts his arms around the till and heaves it with
all his force on to the showroom floor. He is suddenly struck by a
massive, shooting ache in his chest.*

NAT: Oh fuck. Fuck! Gerard!

*He clutches his chest in pain and reels backwards and collapses.
Enter GERARD.*

GERARD: Dad. *(Rushes to NAT.)* Dad!

NAT: Christ it smarts.

GERARD: Sit there, wait there, I'll get help.

NAT: No. I want you to do something for me boy.

GERARD: Anything.

NAT: Take that crowbar and smash the till up. Then burn it.

GERARD: Yeah but you…

NAT: No doctors. I'll tough it out better.

GERARD: But Dad…

NAT: Just do it will ya?! Don't be a wimp!

> *GERARD sighs, picks up the bat, and looks at the till. He raises the crowbar over the till.*

> *Blackout.*

SCENE 2

Flat. LEO is tinkering with the battered and burned till machine. EILEEN enters, putting the finishes touches to laying her dinner table for a large feast.

EILEEN: You're not still fixating over that bloody thing.

LEO: Hey, you'll hurt her feelings.

EILEEN: Please.

LEO: This is a work of art, Eileen, a beauty. She's still got life in her yet.

EILEEN: You're forgetting I grew up with that piece of junk. Sat there in my Granddad's pub jamming every five seconds. It's always been a pile of crap. Why d'you think he gave it to us as a wedding present? Wanted the unwieldy great thing off his hands, so he did.

LEO: Funny. That's what he said about you.

EILEEN: Oi! *(Hitting him playfully.)* Cheeky bastard.

LEO: Come here you unwieldy great thing you.

> *LEO sweeps EILEEN up and kisses her. MICKEY comes in dressed in his Sunday best.*

MICKEY: Uch! Please stop that. Disgusting.

EILEEN: Come here you. *(Spits on her hand and smooths MICKEY's hair.)*

MICKEY: Get off.

EILEEN: There. Now you're handsome.

The door buzzer sounds.

EILEEN: Go and answer the door, make yourself useful.

MICKEY goes.

LEO: It's good of you to do this for Mum.

EILEEN: A thank-you woulda been nice.

LEO: *(Struggles to his feet.)* I'm sure she's touched.

EILEEN: She's touched all right. *(Watches LEO hobble to the drinks cabinet.)* I think you ought to tell them about Western Road tonight. While they're all gathered in one place, get it all out in the open. *(LEO pours the drinks tight lipped. His silence unnerves her.)* Let them know your decision. You're leaving and that's that. It's only fair. You know, then they can, you know, plan for the future. We all can. They'll understand Leo. /In time.

LEO: I haven't secured the lease yet.

EILEEN: What? Are you…are you serious? Why not? Leo.

LEO: I'm dealing with it in my own way, /all right…. *(Buzzer sounds again.)*

EILEEN: Your own way? You'll lose that place if you don't pull your finger out. You will lose that place. Western Road's a wonderful spot. It's perfect, it's right in the thick of it, it's absolutely perfect, you think someone else won't snap it up?

LEO: We just got attacked! All right…/ we just…

EILEEN: Well don't I bloody know it! *(Stifling her emotion.)* For Christ's sake look at yourself. You're lucky to be alive. What if you're not so lucky next time?

YETTA: *(Entering.)* Hello, hello, hello, my Leo, my Leo, he's back. Happy, happy, happy. Look at you. You look well. In the face I mean, don't he look well in the face Nelly?

EILEEN: I've seen worse.

YETTA: Sure, sure, he looks terrific. I knew you'd come t'rough *boychick.* Cos you're tough. Like me. Built to take anyt'ing dey chuck at you. Huh? *(Buzzer sounds again.)*

EILEEN: Can I get you something Yetta? /A drink for yourself.

YETTA: I just wanna look at my Leo. Such a fright you gave us. Right Nelly? Such a terrible fright. But Mama's here now. Mama make it all ok.

Carol enters carrying a cake wrapped up, followed by BERNICE and GERARD. Everyone greets each other with kisses and handshakes. BERNICE ruffles MICKEY's hair.

BERNICE: Who's a pretty boy then?

MICKEY: Get off…

CAROL: Nelly, I brought some pound cake like you told me…

EILEEN takes the cake. NAT enters last on a walking stick.

LEO: There he is! The survivor. *(Starts handing out drinks, starting with NAT.)*

Take more than a dodgy ticker to bring down Nat Solomon, eh?

EILEEN: Look at 'em. The walking wounded.

LEO: Get away, we're in mint condition. In't that right Nat?

NAT: A. One. The both of us. *(Coughs.)*

LEO: That's the spirit. *(Coughs up some blood.)* Fit as fiddles.

EILEEN: Some fiddle. He's been coughing like that since the fire.

YETTA: Fire's a way of life in da rubber game. You pick yourself up. Get back to it.

EILEEN: 'Til the next time.

YETTA: Sure. Dat's what dey say about rubber men. Dey bounce back. Ha?

CAROL: Oh that is funny. That's very funny. *(She laughs like a drain.)*

YETTA: It ain't dat funny.

NAT: Put a sock in it Carol.

LEO hands CAROL a drink.

LEO: Crème de menthe love.

CAROL: Just a few sips.

NAT goes over to the till and looks at it.

NAT: Dear oh dear, this old girl's in a sorry state isn't she?

GERARD: Yeah, sorry about that Uncle Leo.

NAT: *(Clenched.)* Gerard.

LEO: Hardly your fault boy.

GERARD: No...yeah...no I s'ppose not. Yeah.

NAT glares at GERARD furiously.

LEO: Heard it fetched a fair whack in the settlement.

NAT: Weren't too shabby, all in all, I suppose.

LEO: We actually came out pretty well considering. Bloody near saved our bacon.

NAT: Lucky I made sure the insurance was renewed then innit?

LEO: Very. *(Drinks his drink and glares at NAT.)* Almost too lucky.

NAT: What's that supposed to mean?

CAROL: Something smells lovely in that kitchen Eileen.

NAT: Shut up Carol. You got something to say to me Leo.

EILEEN: Actually he does. Don't you Leo?

LEO: Nelly.

NAT: Oh yes?

EILEEN: To all of you.

YETTA: Whaddya got to say den *boychick*?

LEO: I said not yet.

EILEEN: What are you waiting for? They're all here.

Awkward beat. All eyes on LEO. He is silent. Seething with EILEEN.

YETTA: I bet I know what Leo's gonna say. He's gonna say he sees dis terrible disaster as an opportunity. Am I right? As a new beginning.

NAT: Here, here old son. /That's the spirit.

YETTA: As a reminder dat family is all you got in dis world. Dat you gotta stick togedder no matter what. Dat's how we keep strong.

LEO: Well…

YETTA: Am I right?

EILEEN: Leo.

NAT: Very admirable sentiment old son.

YETTA: First t'ing Monday we hit da ground *schprinting*. We get on dem phones, reassure our regular customers dis is business as usual. No changes. Den we dig in. Everybuddy working flat out. Yes? Da kids also, Mickey, Bernice, like in de old days, in de markets. When your Pop was around. You'll see. Even Nat'll roll his sleeves up.

GERARD: And me?

YETTA: What?!

GERARD: You forgot about me.

BERNICE: That's easily done.

GERARD: Shut it you.

CAROL: You did as it happens Yetta. You forgot about Gerard. But I'm sure it was just an oversight love. Wasn't it Yetta? *(Downing her drink.)*

YETTA: Yah yah, sure, oversight, whatever you want. Point is I made a decision. A big decision.

NAT: *(Triumphantly, under his breath.)* Here we go.

YETTA: I decided I'm gonna hand over da business. While I still got my marbles.

NAT: Well if Ma's made up her mind then I, for one, respect her decision.

YETTA: I'm splitting da shop between Leo and Nat. Fifty-fifty.

NAT: What?

YETTA: Straight down da middle.

NAT: Fifty-fifty?

YETTA: Straight down da middle.

NAT: Now wait a minute…

YETTA: Dis is what I decided. / In my head. Yah.

NAT: But who's in charge for Christ's sake? I thought we talked about this…

LEO: Oh did we now?

YETTA: Dere will be no more fighting! OK? No more back stabbing. You're equals now. Brudders. You work like brudders.

EILEEN: Leo!

LEO: There's something I need to say.

YETTA: Wait a minute I'm not done.

LEO: No Ma, I gotta tell you something.

YETTA: I said I'm not finished yet, will you let me finish? Now I know we gotta problem mit space. So, to make everyt'ing easier, I went and got us some new premises.

LEO: You…

YETTA: Smashing little premises on Western Road. Put all da excess stock.

EILEEN: Western Road?

YETTA: It's perfect. Right it da t'ick of it. No more *qvetching* from dat *stitcher*.

EILEEN: I don't fucking believe it.

YETTA: And such a spot. Not surprising dey had udder interested parties. But I out-matched dem. Paid over de odds to get it, yah, but it's ok, de insurance pay-out covers it.

EILEEN: I knew she was up to something. I knew it. That place was for us.

LEO: It's all right Nelly.

EILEEN: It's not all right. It is not all right. How did she even bloody know about Western Road? How?

YETTA: Cos he's my son, dat's how! Cos *I* know what goes on in my own family.

EILEEN: What the hell does that mean?

YETTA: Let me tell you sumtink Nelly, when your family's attacked it sharpens da mind, yah. When you're on da outside in dis world, you protect your turf. Yah. You do whatever it takes. But you protect your family. Leo…he maybe didn't never tell you dis, but when da war was over I got a letter. Tells me da village I came from was wiped off da map. My muter, my farder, my sisters, my cousins… every last one of dem, gone. You know what I did? I tore dat letter up. I got my boys around me and I told dem, I said listen, from now on, dere is no past. Dere is no God. Dere is no *U-manity*. Dere is only us, only dis family, dat's all dat matters. Dat's de only t'ing you can depend on. Everyt'ing else is *dreck*. So we gotta protect each udder. Love…each udder. Cos it all so easy breaks. It all so easy is taken away from you. People…you let dem go…you can't protect dem no more, you see? So we gotta stick… togedder. It's de only way. OK. Now we got dat sorted… let's eat.

Interval.

Act III

SCENE 1

About a year or so later. Street. ROSA enters pushing a pram. WALTER enters behind her.

WALTER: Ronke.

> *ROSA stops. A chill passes through her. She turns. WALTER smiles.*

ROSA: What do you want?

WALTER: *(Gestures the pram.)* So it's true.

ROSA: I…

WALTER: I did not want to believe.

ROSA: Walter…

WALTER: I hoped they were just gossips. Fools. But, no, it transpires, I am the fool.

ROSA: Don't say that. You are not a fool.

WALTER: I want to see him. *(Softens. Smiles.)* May I see the child?

ROSA: He is sleeping.

WALTER: I will be quiet.

ROSA: He has not been well.

WALTER: Is the child not strong?

ROSA: No. Yes. He is fine. Just a little colic.

WALTER: I will be gentle. I just…I want to see him. Hold him.

> *ROSA stares at him, tries to discern how much he knows. WALTER comes closer.*

WALTER: Ronke please…a man learns he has a son, he wants to look the boy in the eye.

ROSA: *(Chilled to the bone at the realisation.)* Oh my God…

WALTER: He wants to behold his triumph.

ROSA: Please…stay back.

WALTER: But Ronke…

ROSA: And don't call me that.

WALTER: I will call you that. And you will call me Wafor. You will call me by my name.

ROSA: I thought we had an agreement. I thought our business was concluded.

WALTER: Our business?

ROSA: Yetta paid you off. She told me.

WALTER: You cannot buy off a father?

ROSA: Oh God, please stop saying that, please…

WALTER: You came to me when you needed help, did you not?

ROSA: Yes. But…look I need to tell you…

WALTER: And I took you in, did I not. I arranged things did I not?

ROSA: You did. Yes. But…

WALTER: And we lived as man and wife? Did we not? And did we not make this child together?

ROSA is backing away now. WALTER approaches, touches ROSA's face. She pulls away.

WALTER: Ronke I have a job now. Hospital Porter. Grim work but I do not mind. Although it degrades a man of my education…/but it is work…

ROSA: Walter…

WALTER: I asked you, now I asked you to call me Wafor.

ROSA: I…

WALTER: Can we please, can we not be ourselves together? / For once.

ROSA: I have to leave now.

WALTER: Just one little peek. Surely, I am owed that. Surely that is the least I am owed.

ROSA: *(Snapping. Cold and tough.)* You were paid what you were owed! Is that not enough for you? Is it never enough?

WALTER bristles. Then takes out money.

WALTER: Then have it back.

ROSA: What is that?

WALTER: Seventy pounds. I paid my debt. Now let me see him.

ROSA: I don't want your money...

WALTER: I said take it woman! And let me see him.

WALTER pushes her out of the way and look into the pram.

ROSA: Leave him alone!

WALTER recoils at the sight.

WALTER: I did not believe. I thought they were fools. I did not believe...

ROSA: I want you to leave us alone. Do you hear me? Leave us alone!

ROSA pushes the pram off. WALTER shouts after her.

WALTER: Does he even know? This man? About his mongrel bastard!

SCENE 2

Three years later. The shop. It is the same premises, with the same counter and the till, but it has been cleared of a great deal of the rubber off-cuts and spruced up a bit. The cushions are now much more vivid colours and designs and there are some additional items in the show room, like bean bags, floor cushions, funkily designed chairs and so on.

It is morning, before the shop has opened. MICKEY enters. He is now in his early twenties. He is well groomed, with tight trousers and a trendy shirt and a pair of Chelsea boots. He walks with a strut as if he is master of this domain, and he carries an era-defining jacket on a hook. He hangs the jacket up on one of the shelves. Then he goes to a switch by the door and presses it on. A neon sign lights up above the premises reading "BEAN BAG SALE TODAY!" MICKEY smiles. Enter MONTY.

MONTY: It's up then.

MICKEY: Yup. Them bags ready? We said by nine.

MONTY: All right, all right, don't be nervy, everything'll be ready.

MICKEY: I can't help it.

MONTY: I'm telling you they'll love it. Trust me. I done some of my best work on them bags.

MICKEY: Good.

MONTY: We're a good team, eh Mickey? Your vision, my skills…

MICKEY: ….finally…finally I'm gonna inject some colour, some fucking sparkle into this dreary old place for once…

MONTY: Nearly nine o'clock, I'll put that sign out.

MICKEY: 'Cos I tell you if this firm doesn't branch out, if we just keep selling bits of rubber, we're finished.

MONTY: S'what I been saying all along…/branch out…

MICKEY: …reticulated foam, strip and cord….mottled chip… s'why I got that crumbing machine…

MONTY: I bloody love that crumbing machine.

MICKEY: We *can-not* be limited to the old ways…the old greys and browns and charcoal blacks…everything grim and grimy…/everything drab.

MONTY: Yes, yes…exactly / exactly what I've been saying….

MICKEY: …I mean, fuck, bean bags is just the tip of it right, I see us doing sofa beds, pouffes in ruffle top fuchsia… aubergine…vermillion…faux leather ones with cow-hide and zebra-skin effect…we could do floor cushions, futons, mattress…all kinds of mattresses. Camp and cot beds, box beds, pocket sprung luxury beds…bespoke, cotton ticking…regular, queen *and* king….and cushions, you know in orange or pink or jade green…semi transparent, yellow violet…pearlsheen in silver pewter and gold, yeah…and it'd be *our* style, a *house* style. See what it's about is people today…people want to…to *individualise… customise*…a home is not just for living in no more, it's about showing the world who *you* are. Yeah?

MONTY: Well yes but hang on…/slow down a minute…that's

MICKEY: I reckon this could get our name into magazines, you know, Sunday Supplements…make us part of the zeitgeist…

MONTY: …right…yes…absolutely…but look…

MICKEY: …look at Vidal Sassoon. This geezer's styling hair like Bauhaus fucking architecture, using *geometric shapes and shit*, changing the whole game. Changing everything. Changing how people look, changing what it means to be young, cos *he* knows; the old ways are finished. The old rules…you gotta smash it all up. Blow it all up.

MONTY: And how are Leo and Nat gonna feel about that?

MICKEY: What? Well…

MONTY: I mean they're working together now, aren't they?

MICKEY: Yeah but…

MONTY: They're in charge, co-directors, /fifty-fifty…

MICKEY: Look, I know all that. /I know all that.

MONTY: And they like things a certain way, don't they, and they don't like change, not one little bit, do they? No sir.

MICKEY: Well no, all right, ok, ok, so I've not quite worked out how to get around that little problem just yet…no, but…

MONTY: *(Chest out, proudly.)* I have.

MICKEY looks squarely at MONTY. Probably for the first time this scene.

MICKEY: You what?

MONTY: I've worked it out. How to get around them.

MICKEY: Oh?

MONTY: *We* set up shop.

MICKEY: What?

MONTY: You and me…couple of machines, I can get a deal on the fabrics…Why not? I been down that basement nigh on ten years Mickey…I been living and breathing this business, I see it first-hand, where we make losses and where we profit. Right? And where we profit is on products that are unique to us. Products that use less material and more creativity. I mean it makes sense…they cost less to make and we can charge more.

MICKEY: You want me to go into competition with my own family?

MONTY: So we set up somewhere else, another borough. It's a big city.

MICKEY: I don't want you to mention this again. D'you hear me? Don't even mention we discussed it. All right? Now get back to work.

MONTY: You got a vision for this place, I know that, but you'll never convince them to change. It goes too deep with them. They'll always hold you back.

MICKEY: It's nearly time.

MONTY: You gotta listen to me Mickey….

MICKEY: I want them bags looking pristine. Right? Everything's gotta be perfect today.

MONTY: If you don't leave now, you never will. Mickey…

BERNICE enters. Provocatively dressed, older and more confident.

BERNICE: Morning!

MONTY: *(Blushing.)* Oh…good…good morning Bernice, you look nice…

BERNICE: You couldn't hang my coat up for me could you Monty love?

MICKEY: Do it yourself, he's got work on.

MONTY: I don't mind. Really. I'm happy to.

BERNICE: There you go then.

MONTY takes the coat from BERNICE and goes out the back.

BERNICE: He's got a little crush on me, that one.

MICKEY: Yeah well keep out of his way, it's a big day today.

BERNICE: I can't help the effect I have on men can I?

MICKEY: What you doing here anyway?

BERNICE: Dad asked me to help out in the office.

MICKEY: Well just keep off the floor, all right, we got discerning punters coming in today. They spy you chewing on fags and flashing your tits, they'll be put off the bags.

BERNICE: I coulda helped sell you know? If you'd only asked me.

MICKEY: Where are they anyway?

BERNICE: Who?

MICKEY: Dad and Nat. It's nearly opening.

BERNICE: Western Road, where d'you think?

MICKEY: What?

BERNICE: Alls I know is they're gonna back and forth all day
so Dad said I gotta man the phones. Said he'd buy me a
new frock for my trouble. Not from a flea market this time,
from a shop.

MICKEY: Back and forth? He said back and forth? Nat and
Leo?

BERNICE: Yes. Why?

MICKEY: Shit. Monty! Get out here will ya! /Monty!!

BERNICE: What's a matter with you?

MICKEY: They can't do this. Not now. Not today. Shit.

BERNICE: Do what?

MICKEY: I spent a bundle on advertising this bean bag sale….
Dad knows that. He knows I'm trying to class this place
up…

GERARD enters in a panic, sweat on his forehead.

GERARD: Right I want this area cleared out soon as.

MICKEY: Oh fuck, I forgot about him.

GERARD: Come on, come on, I need all your gubbins shifted.
/Right now please.

MICKEY: Get out of my face Gerard. I don't need your
nonsense today, /all right?

GERARD: It's not nonsense. Vern's out there right now,
unloading the stock…

MICKEY: What? What stock?

GERARD: What stock? Our stock. What stock.

MICKEY: It's true then. Bollocks. Monty! Get out here!

BERNICE: Why you yelling? What's going on?

GERARD: Stay out of it you. This is business.

MICKEY: They're clearing Western Road. Aren't they?

GERARD: Yes and we got a fuck load of rubber, an absolute fuck load of rubber and it's on its way here and it's gotta go somewhere.

MICKEY: Well it's not going in my showroom.

GERARD: Excuse me? / *Your* showroom?

MICKEY: We got a sale on today, a bean bag sale, have you been paying attention. I need this area clear…/this whole area.

GERARD: The yard's full. The basement's got that bloody crumbing machine you insisted on getting. A small fortune that cost us…

MICKEY: That thing'll pay for itself a /hundred times over…

GERARD: … *I've* been put in charge of the Western Road move, yeah? It's my responsibility to find a spot for the stock, /and I say it goes here.

MICKEY: Yeah it's brilliant you got made milk monitor for the day mate, but I'm trying to save this shop from sinking into fucking oblivion, all right, so would you mind awfully getting your gormless face out of my way?

MONTY: *(Coming back.)* I hung up your coat all nice /Bernice.

GERARD: *(To MONTY.)* Hey! Hey! You! You there. Clear that basement for the stock. Move them tables into a corner, and stick that fucking crumbing machine in the back.

MONTY: What? / Mickey…

MICKEY: Ignore him.

GERARD: Don't ignore me!

MONTY: I'm supposed to get them bean bags pristine.

MICKEY: Exactly.

MONTY: How can I do that if I'm up to my guts in rubber, I can't?

GERARD: All I know is if it can't go in the showroom it's gotta go in the basement.

MONTY: No, no, sorry, no, I gotta put my foot down this time…

BERNICE: Mind out Monty's putting his /foot down.

MONTY: I got a right to breathe like everyone else…/I gotta right to move…

BERNICE: You tell 'em kiddo.

GERARD: Bernice, shut your fat useless gob will you?

MONTY: Uh excuse me, please don't talk to her like that.

MICKEY: Monty's right. You can't go in that basement, we got delicate fabrics coming in, new designs that need care and space, it's detailed work.

GERARD: My Old Man's gonna come stepping through that door any minute. Right? He sees us arguing the toss and not clearing a space for that stock he'll burst a vein in his nostril.

BERNICE: He will. I've seen it, it's already throbbing like Krakatoa.

MONTY: Mickey…

MICKEY: Stop worrying, my Dad'll sort this.

GERARD: I don't think so Mickey.

MICKEY: Leo knows how important this sale is today.

MONTY: You sure about that Mickey?

MICKEY: Course I am, he's not gonna let this dipstick wipe his arse all over it.

GERARD: Oh really?

MICKEY: …he sees you here, he'll bounce you and that rubber straight back to Western Road with your prick between your legs.

GERARD: Oh, well that's funny, that's odd, because the way I remember it, this whole thing was Leo's idea.

MICKEY: …what?

GERARD: I mean, after all, he's the one told us to pack Western Road up, isn't it?

MICKEY: What?

GERARD: Oh my God. Oh wait a second…oh this is priceless…he…he didn't tell you?

MICKEY: What? Yes he…what…course he did, he tells me everything.

GERARD: Oh my. Leo's only played his own boy for a mug.

MICKEY: Christ Gerard I'm gonna batter you…

GERARD: They sold it.

MICKEY: …they…

GERARD: Western Road. It's sold. Gone. Why d'you think we're moving the stock back here?

MICKEY: *(Looks at BERNICE. She looks embarrassed for him.)* Sold?

BERNICE: Business has been slowing down, they wanted to free up some capital.

MICKEY: Business is slowing down because people want more than hunks of rubber. Why d'you think I'm doing this sale?

GERARD: Yeah, well, the sale's off, so…

MICKEY: Says who?

GERARD: I've been put in charge of the move and I say the sale's off.

BERNICE: Well let's all suck off the chosen one shall we?

GERARD: Shut your ugly stinking mouth and get on them phones! I've had with you. /Backchat me?

MONTY: I told you, Mr Gerard, I told you not to talk to her like that.

GERARD: Sorry, am I talking to you? /You nothing piece of *dreck!*

MONTY: I'm simply asking you not to talk to your sister like / that please.

BERNICE: Ooh my white knight.

GERARD: Right you. *(Grabs BERNICE, starts to march her upstairs.)* Get up them stairs!

MICKEY: Oi /oi oi.

GERARD: Get up them stairs you mouthy old slag…

BERNICE: Get off me /you little snot-rag.

GERARD: …get up them stairs and get your fat arse on them fucking phones.

MONTY: I asked you to not speak to her like that. Now I asked you nicely…

GERARD: And you can shut your lip you streak of filth. /You nothing fuck.

BERNICE: You gonna let him treat you like that Monty?

GERARD: Shut your lip. And you get in that basement and get fucking clearing.

MICKEY: Don't you bloody move Monty.

MONTY: I wouldn't move for this ignorant foot-scab if they made him chancellor of the fucking exchequer.

Laughter. GERARD seethes.

MICKEY: That's my boy, Monty. Finally standing up for yourself after all this…

Suddenly GERARD cuffs MONTY hard across the face. Silence.

MICKEY: Jesus.

GERARD: You really… *Christ*. I won't tell you again. You *dreck*! You get yourself down in that…you get down in that…I need that base…fuck!

BERNICE: He's lost it.

MICKEY: What are you thinking Gerard? You don't raise your hand to staff, not a good worker like Monty.

GERARD: I'm his better! He was back-chatting me. *(To BERNICE.)* And you're no better, you cunt-faced cow.

MONTY: Oi! Now I'm asking you nicely… I'm in extreme earnest. I will not tolerate it.

GERARD: This is how family speaks to each other. All right? You don't know because you ain't got one. Now fuck off to that basement you little piss-eyed ponce.

GERARD pushes MONTY. MONTY pushes GERARD.

BERNICE: Oh my God it's a proper rumble. Brilliant.

GERARD pushes MONTY again. MONTY pushes GERARD harder. GERARD falls back in some bean bags. He struggles to get up. BERNICE and MICKEY stifle their laughter.

GERARD: You let him do that to me?

GERARD grabs a piece shelving unit and swings it at MONTY striking him. BERNICE screams.

MICKEY jumps on GERARD and pulls him off, but GERARD tries to swing at MONTY again so MICKEY punches him in the face, knocking him to the floor.

BERNICE: Oh shit Mickey, what did you do?

GERARD: *(Struggling to his feet.)* Shithead. You coulda took my fucking ear off.

BERNICE: Jesus I think he's crying. Let's get some ice on that eye love.

GERARD: Get off. I want Dad to see what he did. In front of staff. /Front of that nothing.

MICKEY: I told you to leave my people alone and you didn't listen. Live and learn.

BERNICE: You're a cocky bastard Mickey.

GERARD: You know what my Dad's gonna do to you for this? Do you?

MICKEY: Well run and squeal to him then cry baby, what you waiting for?

GERARD runs out.

BERNICE: He's right Mickey. Dad's gonna give you a pasting for this.

MICKEY: Nat? He can't even make a fist.

BERNICE: You been throwing your weight around here, sooner or later it's gonna bite you on the arse.

MICKEY: Yeah, yeah... *(Decides something. Goes behind the counter.)*

BERNICE: ...Ordering gear without asking, buying materials, making bean bags.

MICKEY: This sale's been rubber stamped. OK? And you should be thanking me...at least I'm trying to make a go of this.

BERNICE: It's not up to you to do that, you're not the boss here, stop acting like it...

MICKEY: *(Snaps. Furious.)* It's my firm as much as anyone's! *(Back to the counter.)* Fuck are they!?

BERNICE: Listen...go on a delivery, something, just make yourself scarce for a bit, yeah. I'll cover for you.

MICKEY: *(Grabbing a set of keys from behind the counter.)* Got 'em! *(Heads for the door.)*

BERNICE: I'm trying to help you.

MICKEY: They're not getting in that basement. *(He runs out.)*

BERNICE: *(Shouting after him.)* Christ Mickey, don't make things worse!

A moment. BERNICE looks at MONTY and smiles.

MONTY: You all right?

BERNICE: Me? You're the one who got battered.

MONTY: Don't worry about me.

BERNICE: No but…you know…thanks.

MONTY: Nah.

BERNICE: No, you stuck up for me and you didn't have to.

MONTY: He had no right to speak to you like that.

BERNICE: People don't stick up for me as a rule.

Beat. They look at each other.

BERNICE: …way you stood up to him, it was quite something.

MONTY: Anyone woulda done that…

BERNICE: No they wouldn't.

MONTY: Well….

BERNICE: Feel like…you know…I owe you or something.

MONTY: Owe me?

BERNICE: I feel like…you know maybe you should get a reward.

MONTY: No, no. No. Absolutely not. What sort of reward?

BERNICE: *(BERNICE gets closer to MONTY.)* I know you've been ogling me for a while now.

MONTY: Me? Ogling? No, no…

BERNICE: I don't mind.

MONTY: You don't?

BERNICE: No, I like it.

MONTY: You do?

BERNICE: Yeah.

MONTY: Well, maybe I was ogling a bit…

BERNICE: Just a minute. I'll lock the door.

MONTY: What? Why? Oh my God…

BERNICE goes and locks the door and comes back.

BERNICE: There. Bit of privacy. Where were we?

MONTY: I don't know if this is such a brilliant idea…

BERNICE: Oh course it is, no-one'll be in for ages.

BERNICE pulls MONTY over to the counter and then she ducks down under it.

MONTY: Oh God.

BERNICE: *(From below.)* Hello soldier, standing to attention are we?

YETTA appears from the back of the shop.

MONTY: Bernice I really think…I mean it's very thoughtful of you and everth…ooaurrgh Jesus…

YETTA: *(Entering looking at a newspaper advertisement.)* Mickey! You got people talking mit dem signs! You got sumtink going here *boychick!*

MONTY: *(Startled to see YETTA.)* Mrs. Yetta? How did you get in?

YETTA: I wanna see Mickey, he here?

MONTY: No. Ah. Aaaagggh.

YETTA: What?

MONTY: Nothing.

YETTA: What you doing it mit your face?

MONTY: My face? Uhm…eeeuurrggh Jesus.

YETTA: I had enough of dis. Mickey!

MONTY: Oh Jesus Christ.

YETTA: What's a matter everyt'ing's ok isn't it?

MONTY: Oh God. No no…yes no. Yes.

YETTA: Which is it?

MONTY: For God's sake!

YETTA: Right. I wanna know what's going mit you? You gone *peculiar* or what?

MONTY: Uhm…no…oh. Euurgh…I'm fine. Fine. Oh God.

Suddenly there is a knocking at the door.

YETTA: *(Going to unlock the door.)* Who locked da fucking door here?

While YETTA is gone, BERNICE slips out from behind the counter and runs upstairs. MONTY slips back down to the basement. VERN enters carrying rubber sheeting on his shoulder. He has a lit cigarette hanging out of the corner of his mouth. He is visibly in pain with his back.

VERN: What the bloody hell's going on, Mr. Gerard tells me to put the rubber in the basement, I get there, a van's blocking it. What am I gonna do with this lot?

YETTA: I tell you what you do. You put it in your ass. Has everybuddy gone *m'shugah* today or what? *(She begins to head up the stairs.)* I want my Mickey. Mickey!

VERN: *(Dropping the rubber.)* You people are gonna regret the way you treat me!

MICKEY: *(Entering from basement.)* Oi! You can't put that rubber there. Get it up.

VERN: Up down. Tell me where to put it, I'll put it there.

MICKEY: Put it back in the van till this sale's over.

NAT and GERARD enter as VERN, groaning, bends to pick up the rubber.

GERARD: There he is. Tell him Dad.

NAT: Did you move that van?

GERARD: He's trying to keep us out of that basement. That's his game.

MICKEY: Monty's working in there.

NAT: *(Noticing VERN straining to pick up the rubber.)* And what's going on there? Oi Vern! Leave that!

VERN: Leave it now? I'm half way down.

NAT: Get the rest of that rubber out the van.

MICKEY: Don't. I told you to put that rubber back in the van.

VERN looks at MICKEY, then at NAT. Then nods at NAT and goes out.

NAT: Now. Gimme them van keys.

MICKEY: Can't help you, sorry.

GERARD: He's trying to lord it over us. Told you he got no respect. You ask me, he needs his wings clipped.

MICKEY: That van's staying put 'til we've had our sale.

NAT: I want them keys Mickey. /Gimme them keys.

MICKEY: I bust a gut on this sale. You know that. I spent good money. I got a good man down in the basement paying for himself ten times over. I'm trying to save this place and all you two fucking mouth-breathers do is drag me down.

GERARD: I'm getting the distinct feeling he ain't gonna move that van Dad.

NAT: You know why don't you? Cos he's lazy. Like his Lazy Irish Mother.

MICKEY snaps. He throws a punch at NAT, but NAT dodges it.

NAT: Get his arms. Go on.

GERARD grabs MICKEY, NAT pulls a piece of rubber piping from his belt.

MICKEY: Get off me Gerard you shithead.

NAT: That's the way. Keep him straight.

NAT strikes MICKEY in the solar plexus with the rubber piping. MICKEY doubles over. NAT drops the piping and rifles in MICKEY's pockets and takes out the van keys. GERARD punches MICKEY in the face for good measure. Enter EILEEN. She holds a small brown paper bag.

EILEEN: Gerard! Get away from him! Hey! I'll tear this bloody place down. You want to feel my wrath? Do you? Do you want to feel my wrath?

GERARD looks at NAT. NAT nods. GERARD releases MICKEY.

EILEEN: I want to know what goes on here? What goes on?!

NAT: Family business.

EILEEN: God help me, this is my family. Where's Leo?

YETTA appears at the top of the stairs.

YETTA: Hey. What you all standing about for? We gotta sale here in a minute.

NAT: Sale's off. *(NAT then jangles the van keys in MICKEY's face.)* Gerard, move the van. Get that rubber put away. And bin that sale sign.

NAT chucks the keys at GERARD and exits to the back. GERARD exits out of the shop.

EILEEN: Let me look at you.

MICKEY: *(Pushes her away.)* I'm fine. Everything's fine.

EILEEN: You'll need ice on that bruise.

MICKEY: I said I'm fine.

MICKEY pushes past EILEEN and goes to basement.

EILEEN: Mickey!!

YETTA: Leave him.

EILEEN: I can't believe it's happening again. Different generation, but the same fights. I left Belfast to get away from all that. I came here to escape that madness.

YETTA: He'll be fine. He's a good boy.

EILEEN: You think I can't see what's going on here? You think I'm blind?

YETTA: Oh? Do tell Nelly. What's going on in *my* shop?

EILEEN: It destroys the people in it.

YETTA: Oh is dat what you see is it?

EILEEN: I saw this place stifle Leo, break his spirit, I see Mickey going the same way.

YETTA: So what's better, he's a crimper for dem Kensington *Yentas*?

EILEEN: I see you pitting your boys against each other. Keeping 'em under your heal like dogs.

YETTA: Then you don't know nutting! Cos if you knew you'd be on your knees to me.

EILEEN: On my knees?

YETTA: Dat's right!

EILEEN: For what?!

YETTA: His farder was da same, Zikkel. Just da same, I had to keep him on da short leash also.

EILEEN: What are you babbling about now you mad cow?

YETTA: Scrubbers! Dat's what. *(EILEEN is horrified into silence.)* You tink you're so smart, you tink you see it all, but you don't see nutting. You was so keen for Leo to leave here you didn't realise he was gonna leave you too! And *I* stopped him. Cos I know. You save dis shop you save dis family.

After some time.

YETTA: I didn't wanna tell you Nelly. But you made me. So.

YETTA begins to climb the stairs.

EILEEN: You're lying. Yetta!

YETTA: Am I? *(Stopping at the stairs.)* A wife knows. *(She ascends.)*

EILEEN paces. Thinks. Enter LEO, he carries a walking stick, but he's pretty spritely on it.

LEO: Hey you. Ooh it's blist'ring out there. Absolutely blist'ring. Hey what about we nip out, get a choc-ice or something. I missed breakfast.

EILEEN: What? Oh yes I…I know. *(Hands him the bag.)* I brought it.

LEO: Beautiful. *(Takes the bag and smells it.)* What'd I do without you?

EILEEN: Leo…

LEO: Tell you what, we'll share it. We'll take morning off, walk by the river…

EILEEN: I'm gonna make up the sofa. You can sleep on that tonight.

LEO: What? Are you mucking about? Nelly?

Enter MICKEY.

MICKEY: I just want to know one thing.

LEO: Just a minute son.

MICKEY: I wanna know why you ruined my fucking life!

EILEEN: Mickey!

LEO: Watch your lip!

MICKEY: You made me look a chump. /In front of *them*.

LEO: Now look…

MICKEY: You took sides with Nat. You let him bully you into selling that place.

LEO: I think you should calm down.

MICKEY: You're so weak. I despise you.

EILEEN: Mickey!

LEO: I did it for you, you idiot.

EILEEN: ....what?

MICKEY: Me?

LEO: You think I can't see we what's going on? *(Grabs MICKEY's face.)* Looks like he's already caused a fight. *(MICKEY pulls away.)*

MICKEY: I didn't start nothing.

LEO: When the offer came in on Western Road I talked it through with Nat and he agreed. I'm giving my half of the proceeds to Mickey. Start his own place.

MICKEY: You didn't fancy mentioning any of that to me?

EILEEN: That's not how they do things in this family Mickey, they make decisions about your future in secret. They shut you out.

LEO: *(Hands MICKEY a cheque.)* Twenty grand. Start a place. Sell your bean bags. Sell whatever you like.

EILEEN: *(To LEO.)* And what about you? Stuck here still with those two, making your life a bloody misery.

LEO: I'll be fine.

MICKEY: I can't take this.

LEO: Son...

MICKEY: You think I'm letting Gerard take what's mine.

LEO: Forget Gerard.

MICKEY: I won't let him win. *(MICKEY offers the cheque back, but LEO won't take it.)*

EILEEN: Don't sacrifice your happiness for this place Mickey. We had our chance.

EILEEN strokes MICKEY's face and exits.

LEO: Take the money son. Be your own man.

LEO takes down the sign "BEAN BAG SALE TODAY" and follows EILEEN. MICKEY paces, thinking furiously. YETTA appears on the stairs, unseen by MICKEY. She watches him. MONTY comes up with the bean bags.

MONTY: *(Proudly.)* ...rest are downstairs and labelled. All pristine like you wanted 'em.

MONTY sees MICKEY looking at the cheque.

MONTY: What's that?

MICKEY hands the cheque to MONTY.

MONTY: Jesus.

MICKEY: Partners?

MONTY: Partners? What? Serious?

MICKEY: Deadly.

MONTY: Gimme two minutes. I'll get my stuff.

MONTY goes. MICKEY goes to where his jacket's hanging up, takes it off the hook and puts it on. He then starts packing things up excitedly. YETTA comes in.

YETTA: You gotta good Dad dere.

MICKEY spins around to see YETTA above him.

YETTA: Sure, sure, you wanna run t'ings, you wanna be your own man, it's natural.

MICKEY: Why are you still here, you don't work here anymore?

YETTA: Someone's gotta look out for Leo. Now you're going.

MICKEY: He says he'll be fine.

YETTA: Mickey, Mickey, Mickey. I didn't wanna have to tell you dis. *(YETTA now on the showroom floor, throws a glove on the counter. MICKEY looks at it.)* I found it here after da fire.

MICKEY: *(Picks up the glove and looks at it. It has a finger missing.)* Nat.

YETTA: Why you tink I could never trust him to take charge?

MICKEY: No. No, I don't believe it…even Nat wouldn't be nuts enough to do this.

YETTA: If he t'ought it might save da firm…

MICKEY: …Jesus Christ. /Jesus…

YETTA: But whadda you care, you're out da door?

MICKEY: Of course I care.

YETTA: You don't care no more what happens to Leo. You just gonna leave him here. Leave him alone to deal mit Nat and his potz kid, mit no back-up. You're half way out da door. *(MICKEY considers this. YETTA can see she's got him thinking.)* You got what it takes boychick. To drag dis firm into da next decade. You got da vision. Da serkle. Da fight.

MICKEY: I tried to class this place up, they pissed all over it.

YETTA: So you get of da floor and try again. You don't give up. You don't run away. What happens I gave up? Huh? What happens I lose my fight? I die dat's what?

MICKEY: Maybe I'm not you.

YETTA: Don't you say dat. Don't you ever say dat. You made from my flesh and bone. You got my strength in you. You want Gerard to take what's yours?

Enter MONTY with is bag and coat.

YETTA: Ha! Here he is. Anudder deserter.

MONTY: You told her?

YETTA: I treat you like my own blood, you stab me in da back.

MONTY: What? Mickey.

MICKEY: I'm sorry Monty... *(MICKEY tears up the cheque.)*

MONTY: No! Mickey, don't do this, don't let her get into your head.

MICKEY: I gotta stay.

MONTY: Why? What changed? Three seconds ago you were all for it?

MICKEY: I'm sorry, all right? I'm sorry. *(MICKEY exits.)*

YETTA: You heard him. Well. Get back to work. Go on, what you waiting for?

MONTY: No.

YETTA: No?

MONTY: I'm going. Mickey or not, I'm leaving. I got a bit squirreled away. I'll buy a machine...start a place of my own.

YETTA: Start on your own? You? You'll get massacred.

MONTY: I've gotta try Mrs. Yetta. I gotta at least try. *(Starts to go.)*

YETTA: Dis world will crush you. Monty. Monty!

MONTY turns to look at her one last time, then exits. YETTA stares after him. Lights fade down.

SCENE 3.

Ten years later. The shop. Morning. The shop is empty. It has been modernised...a new, electric till on the counter...a lick of paint.... no more string hanging down, no more speaking tubes. It is also in the process of a clear out. Boxes are strewn about, waiting to be removed.

MICKEY is intensely studying the contents of an order books. Enter GERARD with an old sign.

GERARD: *(Picks up an old sign.)* ...look at this. You know Dad drew this? He had real talent back then...before...you know...the incident.

MICKEY: What a heart rending story. Stick on the dump with the rest of the junk would ya?

GERARD: You got no sentimentality.

MICKEY: I want this place to look decent for when Nigel gets here.

GERARD: It's not a done deal yet you know, Mickey. He hasn't bitten yet.

MICKEY: He'll bite.

GERARD: And what about Leo? What if Leo comes to his senses…?

MICKEY: Not this time.

GERARD: We could save this firm. Club together to pay off the lease. /The four of us.

MICKEY: I said I'm not discussing it…

GERARD: Stop Nigel Milton buying the shop.

MICKEY: I don't want to stop him.

GERARD: Why would you let him wipe it all out? Just like that. All them years, our name, kick us out into the street, so he can turn into another one of his ponce-y shops. /Why?

MICKEY: I like his shops.

GERARD: *(Beat.)* He offered you a job didn't he?

MICKEY: I never met the bloke.

GERARD: That's why you won't help us renew the lease.

MICKEY: Keep out of my face today Gerard. OK? I'm serious. Keep out of my face.

GERARD: Leo and Dad can retire, but what about me?

Phone rings.

MICKEY: *(Answers phone.)* Solomon Rubber…. Speaking. No, no, we're all set. Yes, no we're looking forward to Mr. Milton's visit. We're rolling out the red carpet.

GERARD: We coulda worked together Mickey. We coulda done great things you and me. All you had to do was ask me.

MICKEY: *(Scowling at GERARD, but very business-like into the phone.)* Yes, yes, no we're…absolutely, we're rolling out the red carpet.

GERARD: What's gonna happen to me?

MICKEY: *(Covering the receiver. To GERARD.)* I told you to chuck that signage on the dump. Don't make me repeat it.

GERARD grabs the sign and goes.

MICKEY: *(One phone.)* Don't worry the place'll be totally cleared of rubber by the time Mr. Milton arrives. Yes, yes, absolutely, we greatly look forward to his visit. Bye.

During MICKEY's phone call NAT shuffles in looking older, frailer, more vulnerable. MICKEY puts the phone down and starts going through an order book, ignoring NAT.

NAT: That's all my kit cleared out in the office Mickey. End of an era eh son?

MICKEY continues to ignore NAT, looking through his order book.

NAT: I…uh…I left it all spic and span. Marked all them boxes nice for you son…wrote nice and clear so's you know what's what.

MICKEY: Fine.

NAT watches MICKEY awkwardly.

NAT: You had Gerard dump the old signage then did ya?

MICKEY: Yup.

NAT: I suppose you're right, we've had it donkeys years, shouldn't be sentimental.

MICKEY: I wouldn't.

YETTA enters from the back. She is slower, less sure footed, as she shuffles in.

NAT: Only my old man see…in the markets this was, see me and him'd put out them signs first thing every morning… designed the wording together…so…

MICKEY: *(Noticing YETTA.)* What's she doing here? I thought Bernice had her today?

YETTA: I don't need no chaperone you little *pishers.* I'm not *meshugga* yet.

MICKEY: I don't want any of you lot here when Nigel Milton comes.

YETTA: Nigel Milton. Pah. I seen his shops. Nutting special.

MICKEY: He's the leading name in soft furnishings, he's got probably thirty shops.

YETTA: But he ain't got dis one. Not yet.

MICKEY: Just keep off my showroom, all right, both of you.

NAT: Ok Mickey. If that's what how you want it.

MICKEY: That's how I want it. *(Exits upstairs to the office.)*

NAT: *(Calling after him.)* You shout if you need me for anything else son, ok?

YETTA: What is it mit you? Huh? Sixty years dere's been Solomon Rubber, you just gonna give up mit-out a fight?

NAT: Why don't you lie down for a bit eh?

YETTA: Everting I built is gonna vanish like dat. And you're just stand dere like a *schlumpf.* "Oh yes Mickey, shout if you need me Mickey, t'ree bags full Mickey."

NAT: It's delicate, all right.

YETTA: Useless! Always you let me down. Always.

NAT: I'm dealing with it my own way…ok…I'm still a director of this firm.

YETTA: You're not a director, you're a *dreckter.* What happened to you Nat? Huh? You lost your bite. You're toot'less!

NAT: I thought you wanted us to stop fighting? Make peace?

YETTA: Who says fight? Everyting mit you is brute force. Use your *kopf* for once.

NAT: Leave me alone will ya?

YETTA: You got money put away. Right? Rainy day money?

NAT: I'm not touching that rainy day money, that's my pension.

YETTA: A real man keeps going, a real man keeps working till he drops. Our name's gonna be wiped out.

NAT: So what can I do about it?

YETTA: Talk to Leo. Get him to put in more, outbid dis Nigel Milton.

NAT: But I promised Carol…

YETTA: *Carol?*

NAT: …she's got her heart set on this flat in Swanage.

YETTA: Swanage? You want me to vomit? *Carol.* You boys, you couldn'ta picked decent women? Loyal women. Was it so hard? You couldn't do dat one ting for me? After all I done so you didn't gotta fight like me?

NAT: *(Finally snapping.)* But I did have to fight! Over and over again since I was five years old. I did have to fight. Just so you'd *see* me.

YETTA: *See* you?

NAT: Instead of Leo. Always Leo. I worked like a dog in them markets. Looked after that horse. Shovelled its shit every morning. Cleaned up the stall at night.

YETTA: Who needed you? A herring woulda been more use.

NAT: What about this then? *(He shows her his finger.)* Huh? If you didn't *need* me? What's this then?

YETTA: Don't you point dat stump at me.

NAT: You think I forgot?

YETTA: I'm tired of dis.

NAT: No! You'll stand there! For once in your life, you'll stand there and listen! Our call up papers came the same day. That morning I heard you and Pop talking, asking how you'd survive without us. He said the family's finished. The firm...it's finished. He wept. Later...on the stall...it was just me and you...you made me hold a length of tubing. Had to be cut to size. You got a flint and whetted your knife... over and over and you had that look on your face...grim... my heart was racing. You started cutting the tubing...you told me to grip it tight and near the blade...so it didn't slip. But you did slip. It was so sudden. I didn't feel nothing, just saw all the blood. You wrapped my finger in a bit of fabric, told me to get back to work. Suck it up. And I did. I did suck it up Ma. I did a full day, nearly dropped. For you. I went to the recruiting office, they sent me home. Trigger-finger. When I got home I was the one who wept.

YETTA: I gave you dat finger, I can take it back.

NAT: What?

YETTA: What is it, you *wanted* to go to war?

NAT: Leo came back a hero. What have I got? Fifty years of selling rubber.

YETTA: What's wrong mit dat? Dat's an honour.

NAT: *(Sobs.)* I just wanted a chance to prove myself to you.

YETTA reaches out. Almost touches him, affectionately, then thinks better of it.

YETTA: Leo was born tough, everyt'ing bounced off him, but you... Yah you act like da big bear, you growl, you snort, you show your teet', but down deep you're glass. You're mama's little *fegele*. War? You wouldna lasted five seconds. Day one you'da had a target on your back. I'm your mama, I gotta keep you safe any way I know how. I'd kill for you boys.

NAT: Poppa promised me the business. He promised me.

Enter ROSA, older but more comfortable in her own skin. Life has been hard, but not without its small triumphs. She carries an envelope in her hand.

YETTA: Look alive Nat, a customer.

ROSA: I hope I didn't come at a bad time.

YETTA: I know you.

ROSA: I wondered if you'd remember. It's been a lot of years.

YETTA: Yah yah, I know you…

ROSA: I worked here…not for very long.

YETTA: Rosa, isn't it?

ROSA: Yes.

NAT: Rosa?

ROSA: I came because…

Enter TITUS, a fourteen-year-old boy of mixed race, interrupting rudely.

TITUS: It's no good, I can't hold it in.

ROSA: *(Snapping angrily at him.)* I instructed you to wait in the car!

TITUS: I need the bog.

ROSA: Hold it in.

TITUS: I'm desperate. I'm telling you, I'm gonna blow.

ROSA: I told you to go before we left. You never listen to me.

TITUS: You want me to do it right here?

NAT: Toilet's upstairs in the back.

ROSA: Be quick. And less of your cheek.

TITUS runs up the stairs.

ROSA: *(Shouting after him.)* And the word is lavatory! Not bog!

NAT: Kid's eh?

ROSA: I apologise.

YETTA: No, no…he's got life in him your boy.

NAT: What is he, about thirteen?

ROSA: *(Shifts awkwardly.)* Fourteen. *(Notices NAT doing a quick calculation in his head.)* I came here to give you this. *(Hands YETTA the envelope.)* I heard you might be closing, I did not want to miss my opportunity to repay my debt to you.

YETTA: Debt?

ROSA: You helped me…even when you thought I…even when you thought, wrongly, I'd stolen from you. I wanted to show my appreciation.

YETTA looks at the envelope. LEO enters, a slight limp, but still twinkling and buoyant as ever.

YETTA: Leo. Look who's here. Rosa. Remember her?

LEO: *(As ROSA turns to see him.)* Rosa? Stone me…

ROSA: Hello Leo.

LEO: How long's it been? Gotta be nigh on fifteen years.

NAT: Fourteen as it goes. *(Looks at ROSA piercingly.)*

LEO: All this time, eh? You look exactly the same. What you doing back here?

NAT: Repaying old debts. Apparently.

Something about the sneering way NAT has said this chills the atmosphere. But when TITUS reappears on the stairs, it cuts through the tension.

TITUS: You want to sort the flush out in that bog.

ROSA: Titus!

TITUS: *(Cocky.)* Sorry, lavatory.

YETTA: Dem toilets was state of da art in nineteen-forty-seven.

TITUS: Forty seven? They're bloody Neolithic. No wonder they're knackered.

ROSA: Titus!

YETTA: Where does he learn such words?

TITUS: At school.

LEO: That's a bit of a name in'it? Titus.

TITUS: Mum says it's from Shakespeare.

LEO: Very fancy.

ROSA: In Lagos, my father taught English literature.

TITUS: It's a pussy name. I'm changing it soon as I get a chance.

ROSA: You want me to put you across my knee?

YETTA: You know whom dis kid reminds of? My Uncle Pinchas. Back in my village. He was lippy an' all.

LEO: You always said I reminded you of Uncle Pinchas.

YETTA: I did?

ROSA: *(Panics.)* Come Titus, you'll be late for school.

LEO: Leaving so soon?

ROSA: It was good to see you Leo, good to see how this place has changed.

LEO: Dragged into the modern era.

ROSA: Kicking and screaming I suppose.

LEO: Something like that.

TITUS: Needs it. You know how long ago nineteen forty seven was?

YETTA: Whaddya tink I lost my marbles? I know how long ago it was.

ROSA: Titus! That's enough from you! We really must go. Mr. Nat. Mrs. Yetta.

NAT: He's not getting a slice of this shop you know.

LEO: Nat.

NAT: …if that's what you're thinking.

ROSA: I…

NAT: He's not getting cut in. So you can stop sniffin' about for a claim.

TITUS: What's he talking about Mum?

LEO: That's what I wanna know.

ROSA: *(Quietly.)* Don't.

LEO: What claim? She only worked here five minutes.

NAT: Not her. The boy.

LEO: The boy?

LEO looks at TITUS. Looks at ROSA. Reads the truth on her face.

ROSA: Wait outside Titus.

TITUS: Something well dodgy's going on here.

ROSA: I said go Titus! Now!

TITUS: Fine. Yous lot are a buncha whack jobs anyhow. *(He begins to go.)*

YETTA: Wait! I wanna say goodbye to da kid proper. Please.

TITUS: *(Screws up his face.)* What's she on about?

ROSA: Give the lady a kiss.

TITUS: A what?!

ROSA: Don't argue! Do it.

TITUS goes toward YETTA apprehensively. She hesitates, then throws her arms around him.

YETTA: I didn't know.

She lets him go and looks in his eyes.

YETTA: So much like Pinchas.

TITUS: You're a very strange lady. You know they got brain medicines these days?

ROSA: Titus!

YETTA: No leave da kid. He's a good kid. He got spirit. He got fight. He'll be ok, you watch. Go wait outside like your muter says, go.

TITUS: Weirdo. *(He goes.)*

LEO: Why didn't you tell me? Why? Why didn't you come to me?

ROSA: Because I wanted nothing from you. *(Glares at NAT.)* Nor do I now. So you can keep your shop, keep your slices, we don't need them. *(She begins to go.)*

LEO: But can't we at least …can't we…I mean stay for a bit. Let's…

ROSA: I came only to repay my debt. Nothing more. Goodbye.

ROSA exits. LEO stares at the space she just vacated, trying to make sense of things.

YETTA: I'm so sorry *boychick*, I didn't know. I didn't know.

YETTA: I sent her away. I didn't know she was in da family way.

NAT: She'll be back.

LEO: Didn't you hear her?

NAT: You don't believe all that crap do ya? Repaying her debts. She wants a piece of our firm. For the kid.

LEO: What firm? There is no firm.

YETTA: Don't you say dat.

NAT: You're really gonna let Mickey go through with this sale then?

LEO: It's what the boy wants.

NAT: All them years of graft, year after year, building the name. Knocking ourselves out, fighting the competition... all down the drain...all for what?

LEO: What do you want from me? What would you do in my position?

NAT: I'd a taken my belt to that little shit. Long ago.

LEO: Call him that again /I'll take my belt to you...

YETTA: /Stop it you two...

NAT: ...teach him a bit of fucking loyalty.

YETTA: Hey! I said stop it.

NAT: I made sacrifices for this firm! I will not be chucked on the dump like that fucking signage.

LEO: We can't pay the lease Nat.

NAT: We could if we clubbed together. Sold our assets. Re-mortgaged the flats.

LEO: Nelly'd go ballistic.

YETTA: That's not the only reason.

LEO: Shit, how am I gonna tell her...

NAT: You keep it to yourself. We won't tell her. We'll keep your secret. You just help us stop Nigel Milton get his claws into our shop.

LEO walks to the side to think about this.

NAT: Remember the first time we saw this place? It was a shell...Poppa thought we'd lost our minds...markets was what he knew...not bricks and mortar...leases and payrolls...he thought it would bury us. *Meshuganahs* he called us. But Mum persuaded him we could do it. If we all pulled together. We could make a go of it.

MICKEY enters.

MICKEY: What did I say about you lot cluttering up the showroom?

NAT: Well Leo? Go on then.

MICKEY: What? What's he mean, go on, what's going on?

LEO: I suppose I could re-mortgage the flat. Sell the Humber.

MICKEY: What's he on about? What did you say to him?

NAT: I reminded him what he'd be losing.

MICKEY: What?

LEO: There's a lot of history here son.

MICKEY: History?

LEO: You're expecting me to just scrub it all out.

MICKEY: History can't pay the lease. History? History's what's sinking us.

LEO: I want you to make peace with your Uncle.

MICKEY: Dad…

LEO: It would mean a lot to me if you could make peace with my brother.

YETTA: Family is family Mickey.

MICKEY: I can't. You know I can't.

NAT: Shake my hand boy. Admit defeat.

MICKEY: What did you say?

LEO: Go on son shake his hand. Make peace.

MICKEY: Make peace?

NAT: Shake my hand. Show some back bone. Admit you lost.

MICKEY: Don't make me say it Nat.

NAT: Say what?

MICKEY: Don't make me tell him what you did?

YETTA: Mickey?

NAT: What I *did*?

LEO: What you on about son?

YETTA: He don't mean nutting, he don't know nutting…

NAT: He thinks he does. But if he knew anything he'd taken Leo's money and set up on his own. But he didn't did he. Because he's a coward.

MICKEY: But I never burned down my own shop.

YETTA: Mickey!

NAT: What?

MICKEY: I never beat up my own brother.

NAT: You lying little shit.

NAT attacks MICKEY and starts throwing punches. MICKEY is now stronger than NAT, so he easily overpowers him, but LEO throws himself into the fray.

YETTA: Stop it! Stop it you *pishers*!! You maniacs!

GERARD enters carrying a box.

GERARD: Oi oi oi! Get off him!

GERARD drops the box and leaps on top of them. There's a vicious four-way fight, but it's chaos as they blindly hurl punches and shout obscenities.

YETTA: Stop it! Stop! I burned da shop! It was me! I did it! Nat's innocent. So get up of da floor you *schmendriks*!

LEO: *You* did it?

YETTA: I was trying to save us. We was drowning.

NAT: How?

YETTA: I called in a favour dat's how. I came over of dat boat mit all sorts.

MICKEY: You lied to me.

YETTA: You wanna know what it takes to keep dis family togedder? To keep you hooligans in line? Everyt'ing I did, I did for dis family. I did outta love.

LEO: Look at me Mum. Look at me!

YETTA: Don't you tink it kills me to look at you? Every day.

LEO: But it was your doing.

YETTA: You weren't meant to be here. I fixed dat van so you'd be on da road.

LEO: The van?

YETTA: I always protected you Leo. I stood between you and danger. Always.

NAT: What kind of a mother are you? You do that to your own flesh.

YETTA: You gotta see it from my point of view, I had to do sumtink. We was losing business, we was losing everyting. I had to do sumtink.

LEO: Stop it! Stop it. I can't look at you know. /I can't listen to you…

YETTA: I only meant to help…I only meant to help us…like I'm gonna help us now. Yah. You see…you see I talk to dis Nigel Milton. Face to face. I put him straight. I tell him about da rubber game…what dis place means to me. To us. To all of us. I fix dis.

LEO: Don't. Christ. Don't fix anything else. *(NAT suddenly spasms, but LEO doesn't notice and ploughs on).* Just leave us all alone. Leave us alone Mum. Let us deal with this on our own. Let us work it out. Stop fixing things. Stop lying. Stop meddling. Just stop.

GERARD: Dad!?

NAT: *(Clutches his heart.)* Fuck …

GERARD: Dad!

YETTA: What is it, what'sa matter? Nat?

NAT: Christ!

LEO: *(Helping him to a seated position.)* Ok, let's have you here.

GERARD: Oh God...Oh Christ...Dad!

LEO unbuttons NAT's collar.

LEO: Just breathe for me, kiddo.

NAT: Can't....

YETTA: What's happening to him?

LEO: His heart.

MICKEY: Fuck. This is just like him isn't it eh?

LEO: Mickey...

MICKEY: He really picks his moments.

GERARD: Get an ambulance...

LEO: No time. Gerard, get the van, I'll take him down the Homerton.

GERARD goes.

LEO: *(To MICKEY.)* Help me get him up.

MICKEY helps LEO lift NAT to his feet.

NAT: I don't feel so hot Leo.

LEO: Squeeze my hand.

YETTA: ...help him Leo...my little boy.

NAT: My arm. God it smarts.

LEO: Hold on boychick.

NAT: I'm done for. I'm not coming back from this one.

YETTA: Forgive me...I shoulda let you go. I tried too hard. I worked too hard to keep everyt'ing togedder.

GERARD re-enters.

GERARD: Van's outside.

YETTA: Forgive me.

LEO: Gently does it.

YETTA: Forgive me!

But LEO, GERARD, NAT, and MICKEY have gone. Silence. YETTA sighs. Paces, she is struggling, exhausted from the encounter.

Enter MONTY. He is a few years older than when we last saw him and distinguished looking and beautifully, expensively dressed. He smiles at the sight of YETTA.

MONTY: Hello Yetta.

YETTA: Oh. Oh, excuse me, don't mind me. Ok. Yes sir. Whaddya want, darlink, rubber? We got it. Whatever you want, it's made of rubber…

MONTY: No…no, Yetta…it's me. Monty. Monty Minsky.

YETTA: Monty! It's you? Monty?

MONTY: It's me.

YETTA: Well for you I do you a wonderful price. Family discount.

MONTY: Yeah I know all about family discount. That was code for mark it up.

YETTA: Ha. You don't forget it all den.

MONTY: Never.

YETTA: Good boy. I learned you good.

MONTY: You pretty much raised me.

YETTA: Sure, sure, I did. You were a good boy, a nice boy, but delicate. Sensitive. I worried about you out dere. You weren't so tough like Mickey.

MONTY: Well…turns out I did ok.

YETTA: I can see dat. Look at dat suit. Huh? Dat's some serious bit of *shmutah*. You look like you really made somet'ing of yourself, huh?

MONTY: I learned from the best.

YETTA: So you went off, you got a shop, so what?

MONTY: Several shops actually.

YETTA: Several shops. Big deal.

MONTY: Twenty-three to be exact. Worldwide. Twenty-four after we open in New York. Twenty-five…with this place.

YETTA is speechless.

MONTY: Still got that smell, hasn't it? Even with most of the rubber cleared out.

YETTA: …wait a second…

MONTY: Seems bigger too, roomier. Yes this'll make a nice addition to my portfolio.

YETTA: You…I…

MONTY: …turns out I've got a nose for the next trend. I know what'll sell, how to market it. Like a sixth sense. I built an empire on it.

YETTA: You telling me…you're him? You?

MONTY: Nigel Milton. Yes.

YETTA: And you come to buy my shop from under me. Dis is how you repay me?

MONTY: Repay you? Now I want you to hear this because it's important; I'm not that little *pisher* from your basement anymore, I could swallow your firm whole and not break a sweat. Now I came here as a courtesy to Leo and Mickey, but you try to block me, I'll outbid you 'til you weep from your skin.

YETTA: I see it now, I see what dis is. Dis is pay back. Dis is vengeance.

MONTY: You can't live your whole life in opposition Yetta, Christ, it's no wonder we were always breaking for the border.

YETTA: You weren't meant to leave me! Not you. You were da best of dem…it broke my heart.

MONTY: *(Small beat.)* I want the rest of this rubber cleared out by the end of the day.

Broken and beaten, her body slumps as she turns and she shuffles off to the back of the shop.

YETTA: Well. Ok den. Good for you *boychick.* Good for you. What's going around is coming around, ha? Wow, wow, wow….

YETTA exits to the back. MONTY almost tears up. Enter BERNICE from outside, older, dowdy in contrast to her vamp-ish youth. MONTY wipes his eyes, pulls himself together.

BERNICE: Hi there, sorry, I won't be a minute, is no-one here to help you?

MONTY: Hello Bernice.

BERNICE: *(Looks at him, takes a moment to realise.)* Oh my God.

MONTY: I was hoping you'd be here…I…

BERNICE: You did all right for yourself then.

MONTY: I did ok.

BERNICE: Blimey, I feel embarrassed. I haven't…

MONTY: You've got nothing at all to be embarrassed about. Trust me.

BERNICE: Oh…I wouldn't say nothing. *(Smiles, touches MONTY on the arm. He blushes.)*

MONTY: God it's good to see you. I do…I do think about you.

BERNICE: Do you?

MONTY: Do you think about me?

BERNICE: I…I do miss you. You know, being about the place and that. Is that strange?

MONTY: Not at all.

BERNICE: I mean no one ever stood up for my honour before…or since really…

MONTY: I was hoping we could catch up, get a drink maybe.

BERNICE: God I'd love that…

MONTY: Really? I mean cos we could…

BERNICE: Thing is I'm…I got Bert…so…

MONTY: Bert?

BERNICE: My husband.

MONTY: Oh.

BERNICE: Three kids. So…

MONTY: Jesus. You've been busy.

BERNICE: …it was a nice thought though. A really nice thought.

Their eyes meet. They smile. There is a charged moment between them…MICKEY enters watches them drawing closer.

MICKEY: Shit a brick. Monty?!

MONTY and BERNICE break apart.

MICKEY: Bern, you gotta get down the hospital. Nat had a turn.

BERNICE: Oh shit. I gotta go. Sorry love I gotta…shit.

MONTY: Of course. Go.

BERNICE touches MONTY, kisses him, and then runs out. MICKEY looks at MONTY. Realises.

MICKEY: Blimey have a look at these threads. You did all right didn't ya?

MONTY: What's wrong with Nat? His heart?

MICKEY: Look, I'd love to stay and chat about old times, I really would mate, but I got this big cheese coming today, really big cheese. If I tell you his name you won't believe it.

MONTY: I'm glad you're finally cutting loose Mickey. It's the right decision.

MICKEY: Oh. You heard?

MONTY: I been keeping my eye on this place for a while.

MICKEY: You what?

MONTY: The area's on the way up. Gentrification, regeneration, you musta noticed? Five years, this place'll be worth a mint. That's why it's the right time.

MICKEY: The right time?

MONTY: For a first-class soft furnishings outlet.

MICKEY: What's going on here? You winding me up?

MONTY: Did you never wonder what happened to me when I left here?

MICKEY: Well yeah of course, but...

MONTY: It was hard. Really hard. Touting for work, no one to catch me...

MICKEY: Monty, mate...

MONTY: But I was driven. Had to be. Had to live. Mended anything I could, cheap as I could, throws, curtains, cushions covers...till I had enough for a place. Things went all right...Then one day I came up with my idea. Give Englishness back to the English. Every conceivable soft furnishing in tweed or canvass...countryside colours. Racing Green, Mustard Yellows...Heritage Red, Periwinkle, Air Force and Blizzard Blue. But in my style, a House Style.

MICKEY smiles at the recollection.

MONTY: I had to change my name of course. Something more Anglo Saxon.

MICKEY: *(Smile vanishes.)* Wait you're...what are you telling me? That you walked out of here a little *pisher* and went and conquered the fucking world? That you're him?

MONTY: You had my back when I was here. I never forgot that. But also you saw the future. And you showed me that future. I could use that vision in my organisation.

MICKEY: Wait a minute, I don't /know about this...

MONTY: Everything's possible now. The future's up for grabs, it's uncertain, but it's ours if we want it. The red tape's been slashed, the shackles are off. It's a brave new world. Finally, we can build, expand. No limits. Don't get left behind Mickey. *(Pause.)* There's a new wine bar on Seaton Street, where the iron mongers used to be. Meet me there we'll work out the details. Then we'll toast to success. No, not success...freedom.

MONTY goes. MICKEY ponders. Then, suddenly, with great purpose and a rush of euphoria, he pulls his keys from his pocket, slams them on the counter and runs out, calling after MONTY. YETTA appears holding a can of kerosene and pouring it around the shop.

YETTA: I'll burn dis place down before I let you take it! How'd you like dat in your portfolio, you *stitcher*?! Nigel Milton. Don't make me laugh. *(She stops. Can't do it. Drops the can.)* I can start again. Ya. I don't need nobuddy. I build it all up again from nutting. You want fight, I show you fight. You tink I'm finished? I'll show you how to fight you *stitcher!* I'll show you how to live!

End of play.

ACKNOWLEDGMENTS

The author would like to thank Ed Hall, Greg Ripley-Duggan and all at The Hampstead Theatre. Nicholas Hytner, Sebastian Born, Mark Rosenblatt, David Horovitch, Ben Power, Laura Collier and The National Theatre Studio for workshopping the early drafts of the play. The invaluable books *Bloody Foreigners, The Story of Immigration To Britain* by Robert Winder, *Thinking The Twentieth Century* by Tony Judt with Timothy Snyder, *No Such Thing As Society, A History of Britain In The 1980s* by Andy McSmith, and *Them and Us, Changing Britain – Why We Need A Fair Society* by Will Hutton. Also, Richard Bean for threatening to write this pay if I didn't, Chetna Pandya, Rebecca Mills, Allan Swift, Simon J Ashford, Roger Goldby, Rose Cobbe, James Hogan and all at Oberon Books.

This play is dedicated to my parents.

WWW.OBERONBOOKS.COM